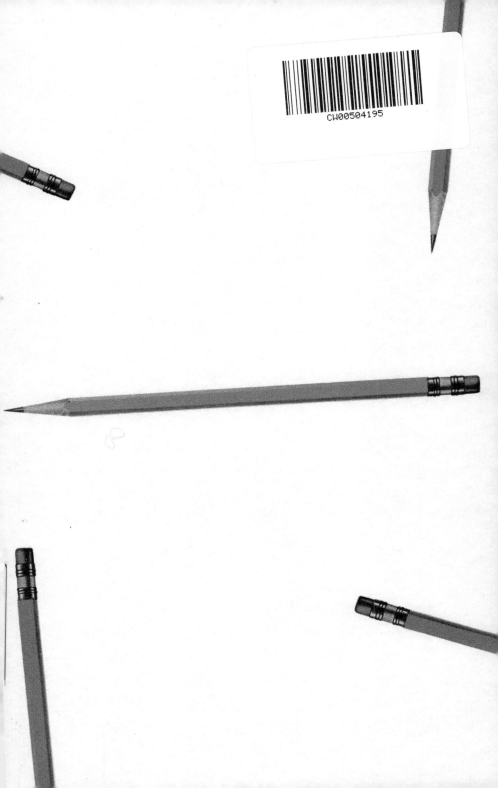

PLEASE MISS, WE'RE BOYS

To Nadesha and Heathie with
best wishes
Susan Elkin   Sx

Susan J. Elkin

The Book Guild Ltd

First published in Great Britain in 2019 by
The Book Guild Ltd
9 Priory Business Park
Wistow Road, Kibworth
Leicestershire, LE8 0RX
Freephone: 0800 999 2982
www.bookguild.co.uk
Email: info@bookguild.co.uk
Twitter: @bookguild

Typeset in 11pt Adobe Garamond Pro

Printed and bound in the UK by TJ International, Padstow, Cornwall

ISBN 978 1912881 529

British Library Cataloguing in Publication Data.
A catalogue record for this book is available from the British Library.

For the boys of 1B, wherever they are today.

CHAPTER ONE

Testosterone has a lot to answer for. But in 1968 I'd never heard of it. I rather thought that boys were pretty much like girls, except for a few additional lumpy bits for decoration – and, maybe, one or two other little purposes.

No one told us in my girls' grammar school that teenage boys, and maybe many adult men too, think about sex almost all the time. Of course we thought about it a lot ourselves too, but few of us even understood male anatomy, which was mostly sidestepped in our otherwise pretty comprehensive biology lessons. You can glean only so much from classical statues such as Michelangelo's David. And we certainly had little idea how teenage boys functioned in terms of urges, fantasies and preoccupations.

When I was in my early teens, around 1960, parents and magazines primly warned us all the time that men and boys behave like gentlemen only if you conduct yourself like a demure lady. Never must you lead a man or boy on because no one belonging to the male sex can control himself. That's how he's made. He can't help it. No blame attached. If the 'worst' – i.e. sex, pregnancy and/or some hideous incurable disease – happens, it is entirely your fault not his.

And, of course, ladies – we were told – don't themselves feel any sort of sexual desire unless they are safely married and even then sex is probably a bit of a bore that you have to put up with. My own, apparently happily married, grandmother was wont to boast openly, without seeming to see anything remotely odd in

1

it, that my grandfather had never seen her naked. A lifetime of reluctant fumbles under the sheets seemed to be, for many, quite normal.

So, one way and another, I'd led a pretty sheltered life. There were no male staff at Westwood Grammar School for Girls, part of a group of girls' schools founded in the nineteenth century for the daughters of gentlemen who were progressive enough to want affordable education for their girls as well as for their boys. When I started at Westwood in 1958, the atmosphere was almost conventual, except that by then some of the staff were married, which wouldn't have been the case a few years earlier. The only male on site was the resident caretaker, and I think his tabby cat may have been a tom.

Precious little opportunity to learn about men at school, then. The Headmistress, Miss Amy Harper, an Oxford graduate in English and very knowledgeable about Beowulf, Dryden and English grammar, obviously, was as sexually naïve as we were. Presumably her studies hadn't included *The Miller's Tale* or D. H. Lawrence. And I suppose all her Shakespeare was bowdlerised, so she'd never even met the porter in *Macbeth* with his clear case of brewer's droop.

When one of our number did actually, horror of horrors, 'lead a man on' and become pregnant, the social worker (who happened, much later to become my mother-in-law) came to see Miss Harper to discuss the girl's future education and options. Our blinkered Headmistress simply wouldn't countenance the pregnancy as a reality or problem. 'Oh no, none of my girls would behave like that,' she said, insisting, in all seriousness, that the social worker had made a mistake and come to the wrong school.

On another occasion, a year before I left, a fellow sixth former became pregnant and quit school to get married – a popular, hasty solution in the '60s. Miss Harper and several other staff, to our amusement and incredulity, announced the impending nuptials as a piece of interesting, if faintly surprising, good news, an achievement like passing a music exam or winning a tennis tournament. Almost unbelievably, none of them seemed to know why the girl was suddenly giving up A Levels, and nearly everything else, in order to hasten to the altar instead of university, teaching or nursing. I hope, a year or two later, they read Margaret Drabble's 1965 novel, *The Millstone*, about a young woman who became inconveniently pregnant. It could have been written for them.

So, educated in that environment – although a bit more worldly than my teachers (I'd read *Lady Chatterley's Lover* by then, after all) – I had, when I started teaching in 1968, a lot of ignorance to slough off. And the male adolescents of Deptford, where sex simmered continuously just below the gritty, grimy surface, were eagerly waiting to educate me.

The learning started on day one.

'Well, I never thought you'd turn up,' said the benign, balding, bespectacled sixty-something man I had innocently assumed was going to interview me for my first proper job. He clearly knew a lot of things Miss Harper didn't, which is why he was surprised.

Harry Baker surveyed me quizzically over his glasses before hurrying round his desk and across the dark, rather dingy room he had for an office. Then he smiled. Perhaps it was my shortish, bright orange 1960s interview dress. Or perhaps he hadn't spoken to a woman under fifty for a while.

Actually, I realised much, much, later he was, at that moment, offering silent prayers of thanksgiving to the God of Headteachers. Divisional Office had sent him a reasonably normal, able-bodied young teacher who might, just might, turn out to be the answer to a prayer and grow into someone who could fill one of the numerous staffing gaps in his 'challenging' – very challenging – South London boys' school where the testosterone flowed in the gutters and nearly everywhere else.

Who knows? Mr Baker was thinking, forty years of experience behind him and between him and me, as he showed me courteously downstairs to the playground where he parked his car, a weathered, unhurried Ford Consul – rather like its owner. And the fact that I was young, female, pretty wet behind the ears – and therefore a most unlikely contender – didn't seem to faze him. In fact I suspect I was an exotic novelty and therefore rather appealing. Not quite a Mary Quant-style dolly bird perhaps, but I didn't look too bad by Deptford standards.

He drove me gently across grubby, but colourful, Deptford to another school. And that was my first puzzle because I thought, not unreasonably, that I had presented myself for interview at the school in which, I thought, I might be offered a job.

But nothing, nothing at all, was as it seemed, neither then nor for the rest of the five years that I worked at the masculine, if not muscular, Creekside Comprehensive.

It was June 1968 and I had just completed a pretty useless, head-in-the-clouds-but-rarely-in-the-classroom, three-year teacher training course at an airy-fairy college on the south coast. Then it was simply a teacher training institution. Today it is part of a local university.

It was a mixed college, but its Church of England history meant that many of the male students were rather staid, clean-living types. Of course there was some 'going out' and a great deal of sitting around in each other's rooms in groups setting the world to rights – although only until 11pm when, boarding school style, we all had to be in our own hostels unless we'd been issued with a late pass. It was an expulsion offence to be caught in an opposite-sex hostel after 11pm – as if sex only takes place in the night. In my third year I spent a fair amount of time doing exactly what the staff were trying to prevent me from doing in my own student hostel room but only until 10.55pm. And, for the record, only with the man I married a few months later. It was hardly edgy 1960s living and it taught me little about men and boys in general.

Now I was back in my native South London, only three years after leaving Westwood and Miss Harper's blinkered outlook on life, in search of a job.

The Inner London Education Authority was just three years old, having in 1965 replaced the old London County Council of my childhood. 'London County Council, LCC, Put a penny in the slot and out goes he' we used to chant in my primary school playground before I passed the eleven plus and my parents chose Westwood for me from the half a dozen or so good, local grammar schools for girls who were deemed bright, or brightish.

Under the bright shiny new ILEA – finally put to rest by the Conservative government in 1990 – London was arranged in a number of divisions. And if you were a newly qualified, wannabe teacher you had to apply to the local divisional office rather than to a school.

The day before my meeting with Mr Baker I had been at a cattle-market-style interview at Division 7's HQ, which was in Greenwich High Road in a nice, old, red brick municipal building. It's still there, long since redeployed of course, looking pretty shabby these days.

I waited with several other 'girls' to see the Divisional Officer (D.O.). We were each aged twenty-one and all recent completers of teacher training courses. No one would have called us 'graduates' in those days because we hadn't been to university. Had I then known the word 'clone' in 1968 I would have felt like one.

Eventually it was my turn. After a few desultory questions we got to what was really worrying Mr Divisional Officer. And it was triggered by the engagement ring on my finger.

I had been friendly with Nick, the young man I was intending to marry, since I was fourteen and he was sixteen. His background was very much like mine and he'd attended a boys' grammar school a mile or two from Miss Harper's establishment. We'd met at a church youth club. Both our families had been churchgoers for generations but he and I had both permanently abandoned the church and its doctrines by the time we got together properly during my second year at college. Once Nick, who worked for Lewisham Borough Council, got his first car – a splendid grey

Morris 1000 – he used to drive down to see me at weekends and, gradually, one thing led to another and we fell in love.

South London is like a village and there are many connections amongst families who have lived there for a long time. When Nick first started dropping into our house when I was fifteen or so, my father suddenly said, 'Did you say that boy's name is Elkin? My brother and I knew a Roy and George Elkin before the war. We all went to scouts together and were really close friends. I bet he's the son of one of them.'

And so it turned out. Nick is the son of George Elkin who'd been my uncle's best friend in the 1930s. Even my grandparents remembered the Elkins fondly and when, eventually, Nick and I got engaged and got them all together after a gap of more than twenty-five years, we just slunk away and left them to their reminiscing. I was, therefore, effectively marrying the boy next door and all parties were delighted. As far as my father and his father and brother were concerned, Nick came from excellent stock and I could do no better.

Not that Mr D.O. needed to know any of this. His mind was on employment issues. Political correctness and equality in the workplace lay far into the future. Although Miss Harper was, in her sexless, letters-in-*The-Times* way, quite a champion of proper opportunities for women in, for example, medicine and law, many people still thought there was no point in educating women because it would all go to waste when they became full-time wives and mothers. Real, radical feminism was just a twinkle in Germaine Greer's eye. It would be another two years before we got her provocative book, *The Female Eunuch.* So Mr D.O. was definitely allowed to ask his M question in 1968.

'I see you're getting married,' he said bluntly and without warmth. 'How long do you plan to carry on teaching?' He meant did I intend to give it all up and morph into a 1950s-style, duster-wielding housewife as soon as I'd taken off my wedding dress. Or, worse, what about babies?

Of course I said the first thing that came into my head, fortunately having always managed to sound firmer and more assertive than I am feeling inside. Germaine Greer might have been quite pleased with me.

I told him that I had become engaged the previous year to a local Lewisham boy whom I had known for several years, that we were marrying in the following spring and that I intended to go on teaching for a very long time. Teaching was definitely my priority. Oh yes, I would, I promised glibly, be a reliable long-term teacher.

Oddly enough that turned out to be the truth although, of course, not being clairvoyant, I didn't know it, or even believe it at the time. I taught for thirty-six years and, one of the first beneficiaries of the new entitlement to maternity leave, managed to be on somebody's payroll somewhere for the entire time, except for three weeks when we moved to another area and that's how long it took me to find another job. But all that was several years down the line.

It must have satisfied Mr D.O. in 1968, though, because he then reached for a file on the corner of his desk and said portentously, 'Well, in that case I think I've got the perfect opportunity for you.'

He continued, suddenly full of upbeat warmth which, if I'd been older or more experienced, would have made me very suspicious: 'It's a local school just up the road from here. It's all boys which I think will suit you, and the Head, Mr Baker, is an old friend of mine. Would you like to go and see him tomorrow?'

With hindsight it was like that wonderfully triumphant, but loaded, line W. S. Gilbert gives KoKo in *The Mikado*: 'Congratulate me, gentlemen, I've found a volunteer.' Why on earth would anyone think with my education I could possibly have been especially suited to working with all boys? Perhaps he was looking at my well-above-the-knee 1960s dress and thinking… well, the sort of thing I was soon to learn that boys and men think about all the time.

Before I could draw breath to answer, he was reaching for the phone and happily informing Mr Baker of Creekside Comprehensive that he had a Miss Susan Hillyer in his office, an enthusiastic young teacher who was very keen to come and meet him the next day. Much later I wondered if he phoned again after I left to speak to Mr Baker rather more frankly and if so what was said?

This ILEA system for new teachers was not unlike a medieval hiring fair for agricultural workers. Once accepted by Divisional Office, recruits were despatched to needy schools in the division. It meant that you could be moved to another school without notice if things didn't work out or if there was an even greater shortage somewhere else.

In practice, as long as your face fitted and you didn't do anything criminally stupid, you more or less became part of the school you were sent to. Then, after a year or so, you might be upgraded to assigned staff status, which meant you had permanent tenure in the school and couldn't be moved at the drop of a hat.

So there I was, sent by Divisional Office and driven across Deptford to the section – known as Lower School – of Mr Baker's Creekside Comprehensive where he needed bodies in classrooms. Urgently. And if it was a female body, in that testosterone-heavy environment, then so much the better. Mr Baker, after all, had once been a teenage boy himself and knew plenty that I didn't.

So desperate was he for bodies in classrooms that I was about to benefit from a wonderful wheeze dreamed up by the ever-resourceful ILEA, which had to find ways of hooking young teachers, of which it was always short.

Although I had already finished at college – and then enjoyed a memorable week's holiday in Norfolk with Nick – the school term still had five weeks to run. I could, Mr Baker explained persuasively, start the following Monday. Because my exam results were not yet through from college, I was technically unqualified so I would be paid two thirds of a normal starting salary. Not a bad rate of pay for someone who was still really a student. Much better than bar work.

But – and this was the wheeze – if I agreed to work at the school indefinitely from September, by which time I'd be officially qualified, I'd then be entitled to the other third of my summer term salary – backdated and paid as a supplement to my first month's salary.

It was an offer I couldn't refuse although, had I been older and wiser, I might have wondered just why the school, and ILEA, were so anxious to recruit me?

Lower School was where the 11-14-year-old boys and their rampant hormones and wet dreams were based. It was the section of the school which would now be called Years 7-9 or Key Stage 3, when boys hit puberty head on.

Upper School, where Mr Baker had his office, and all the heads of department ran their little empires, operated as an almost completely separate entity at the New Cross end of Deptford. At Lower School, almost a mile away, we were nearly in Greenwich.

And it was to Lower School that Mr Baker drove me on that first day.

It was a rather strange, but elegant in its way, long thin building dating from the 1930s. It lay close to the pavement and stretched almost the entire distance along the main road between two side turnings 300 yards or so apart.

Behind the school was a vast playground – gruffly known as 'the yard' to most of the staff. Most of the building was just one room deep and the teaching rooms faced the playground on three storeys. Three very long corridors ran through each of the three storeys behind the classrooms with a staircase at each end and one in the middle.

The school keeper, as caretakers were then known, lived in a detached house in the middle of the yard with his back garden extending to the perimeter wall of the playground. Goodness knows what it was like in there for his home-based wife during breaks when the entire school, rain or shine, was turned out into the yard. Perhaps she timed her shopping excursions to miss them. Like me, she must have felt pretty lost in that sea of males.

At the far end of the yard sat a series of single-storey, self-contained huts where, I soon discovered, men of varying character and reputation taught crafts such as plumbing and brickwork.

The stately, gentlemanly Mr Baker drove me towards all this into the playground via a side street entrance and then diagonally across the yard to park near the building. Fortunately there were no yelling, football-kicking boys to run over because all were in lessons at that moment.

The front of the school, which faced the main road, and the playground were connected by a large pedestrian archway which penetrated the building halfway along its length. The unpretentious main entrance – just a door – was beneath the archway on one side and you could get to it from either street or playground.

Also under the archway was the horror of the boys' toilets – my first real encounter with maleness in the raw. Now, if these facilities were ever cleaned or disinfected, I never saw or smelt any evidence of it in the whole five years that I worked at the school.

The ammonia-scented stench and reek of filth assailed you from fifty paces. It made the *pissoirs* of the Parisian streets seem, by comparison, like somewhere you might happily eat your picnic. And you had to brave these fumes and walk past the entrance to these 'facilities' in order to get into the building – whether you were a parent, inspector, staff member, pupil, visitor or prospective new teacher.

A metaphor, perhaps, for some of what lay inside? Or maybe it was a test. If you can pass our bogs and stay upright you'll be a man (or woman), my son. Either way, clearly no one on the staff had ever read or thought about that old saw: 'You never get a second chance to make a first impression.'

Yet, amazingly, it didn't put me off. My grammar school had clean, ladylike indoor toilets. I had no brothers, or even male cousins. Westwood had striven quite hard to keep us away from boys, not least because it might have distracted us from the serious business of learning and passing exams. My experience and knowledge of boys and their habits was limited to the handful of wholesome grammar school types, like Nick.

When I first smelt those bogs at Creekside Comp, I honestly thought – in my youth and ignorance – that this must be what boys en masse were like. I presumed – concluded, accepted – that they pissed all over the floor, the walls and each other and that this was probably normal. They, and their lavatories, would be bound to smell and if you worked with these male treasures you had to train yourself to imperviousness. All this I decided in a split second.

So Mr Baker and I walked from the playground under the arch, past the redolent toilets, which I pretended not to notice and he presumably really didn't because he was so used to it, and into the building.

There was no reception area in schools in those days. And no security locks either. Anyone could have strolled in and occasionally undesirables of various sorts did. Mr Baker led me ponderously up the central stairs to the first – middle – floor and the heart of the school – although it wasn't remotely hub-like or dynamic.

It consisted of a small office for the Head of Lower School and a tiny room in which two secretaries worked – the sum total of the school's admin staff. On one side of the Head's office was a staffroom and on the other a library. On the other corner of the stairwell were the adult male toilets. No smell. Presumably the staff had better aim. There was also a little kitchen for the all-essential brewing of staff tea.

'Meet Jim O'Riordan, Deputy Head of Lower School,' said Mr Baker.

'Hello,' said Mr O'Riordan, sizing me up eyes a-gleam. 'Are you able to start on Monday?' he added. 'If so, there are three people we must introduce you to.'

Tact. Had I but known it then that even amongst boys' schools this was the 'roughest and toughest' for miles around. The staff were (almost) all male. I was twenty-one, female and green as grass. It was most unusual in 1968 for such a school even to consider taking on someone like me.

But there was another woman, French by birth but married to a Brit. She taught French part-time. Heloise Scott was a few years older than me – perhaps thirty. Then there were Janet and Margaret, the two middle-aged secretaries. Apart from Mrs Port, who came in three times daily to make staff tea, and some of the cleaners, the four of us were the entire complement of female staff.

Heloise and I had to use the single loo (and we didn't piss on the floor either) which opened off the back of Janet and Margaret's little office because there were no other facilities on the premises for women.

It was these three female comrades-at-arms, Heloise, Janet and Margaret, that Mr O'Riordan, sensibly, wanted me to meet before I left that first day. It might have been appropriate to have shown me round the school or talked to me about what they wanted me to do for the rest of term. But no one did. Perhaps they were afraid that if they showed me too much, I'd take fright and bolt.

Instead, I hopped happily on a bus and headed for home, full of glee, to tell my parents the glad tidings that I was employed – as a teacher! Just as I'd been saying that one day I would be since my father had taken a photograph of me, aged three, teaching my dolls in my grandparents' garden.

'Well, if you cope there, girl, you'll cope anywhere,' said my father with his usual laconic wisdom.

He knew a thing or two about teaching and Deptford did my father, although even he didn't warn me about teenage boys and their irrepressible sex obsessions. After serving in the RAF in World War II he had done one year emergency teacher training and then gone to teach maths and PE very successfully at a rather unusual mixed grammar school at the other end of Deptford High

Street, half a mile or so from my new job. He taught there for several years before leaving the profession to start his own business.

He always insisted that I came from a 'teaching family' anyway. His own father, my grandfather, had also done emergency teacher training – after active service in France in World War I. Grandfather was a primary school teacher at various schools in South London for forty-six years, having started in the 1920s at a school in Peckham not far from my new job. He had returned to teach part-time after his retirement in 1958, and had been forced by cancer of the throat finally to stop only a year or two before my arrival in Deptford.

So there I was, continuing the family tradition. Same job. Same area. And eagerly looking forward to Monday in blissful ignorance of the testosterone-fuelled waves I was about to create in that school.

CHAPTER TWO

My first problem was very basic. Where was the school exactly and how was I supposed to get to this, as I still romantically thought, quaint establishment for boys? I'd gone by train to New Cross for the interview and didn't know Deptford well enough to be fully aware of where I'd been driven by Mr Baker.

Much studying of the London A-Z ensued. As did discussion with my father, a life-long South Londoner, and with Nick who, as a Lewisham Borough Council employee, knew the whole area pretty well.

Lower School was on the Deptford and Greenwich border and a bit off my radar. In the end I plumped for a walk to Catford and a bus through Lewisham to Greenwich followed by a walk up Creek Road. Not a particularly convenient journey.

I didn't have many clothes in those days. I was barely out of studenthood, after all. The summer dress I'd worn to the interview had cost thirty-two shillings and sixpence (just over £1.60 in modern money) a couple of years before and I didn't want to be seen again in it immediately. For my first day on the job I wore a shortish dark blue linen skirt a friend had made me – with sandals and a short-sleeved blouse. Everyone – even the Queen – wore relatively short skirts in 1968, but mine were nothing like as short as many women's. I'd always been prone to plumpness and was conscious that short suited me much better than mini, so none of it was too revealing by the standards of the day. Neither of my parents thought to suggest that if you're going to work in a boys' school in Deptford you need to be very careful about how you dress and present yourself because teenage boys, especially when shut up all day in an all-male enclosure, are likely to be rampant sexual fantasists.

I set off at 7.30 having bought a copy of *The Times*. A little bit of self-assertion because my parents were *Daily Telegraph* readers and I thought *The Times*, with its strange, advertisement-covered front page, was rather more grown up. I read my newspaper on the bus as I set off on that first Monday. A journey into the unknown – the mentality as well as the geography.

Mr Baker was at Lower School to meet me. He was obviously taking my starting at his school surprisingly seriously and doing his best to ease me in that first day – although of course, I didn't realise that at the time. He looked at me – with my long glossy dark hair (those were the days) and blue skirt – with enthusiasm and approval.

I soon learned, though, that his presence at Lower School was unusual. It was quite normal for him not to be seen there for days at a stretch. Lower School was for him, and his senior colleagues, generally beyond the pale. As far as they were concerned, the important stuff happened in the other building.

A number of the staff were away, Mr Baker explained to me, on a school trip. They had taken a large group of second-year boys to Sayers Croft, a residential field centre in Surrey, then owned by ILEA. So the school was fairly quiet.

But what about the flotsam and jetsam who, for some reason (likely to misbehave, molest some hapless female, go thieving, uninterested in anything to do with school, parents who wouldn't/ couldn't pay the modest charge?) had not gone to Sayers Croft? The group was gone for nearly two weeks and something had to be done with the remnants.

I should have seen it coming but of course I didn't.

Creekside Comp used a rigid streaming system. On arrival in the school, boys were divided into classes in which they did all their lessons. These groups were then unapologetically labelled 1A, 1B and so on down to 1F or sometimes 1G depending on the numbers in the year. Self-esteem and concerns about it had not, definitely not, been invented.

We were, in name and theory at least, a comprehensive school, so there should have been a goodly number of highish flyers in the upper streams. Actually most of the brightest brains were in the local grammar schools, of which there were plenty in South London in 1968. Grammar schools, like the one I attended, weren't finally phased out of ILEA – to be subsumed by comprehensives, go fully independent or close down – until the late 1970s.

There were also a few parents who fell in love with the Great Comprehensive Dream in its earliest form and decided, for ideological reasons, to send their children to schools such as Forest Hill School. Forest Hill was a purpose-built, state-of-the-art comprehensive school for boys, which opened in 1956. Several of the boys in my primary school class – who'd all passed the eleven plus – went there proudly in 1958. Other shiny comprehensives in the area included Kidbrooke, near Blackheath, and Kingsdale in Dulwich. Failing such sexy options, as a last resort, such blinkered parents sometimes sent their offspring to Creekside Comp. But there weren't many of those.

One boy, who hadn't done particularly well at primary school, told me years later that his middle-class parents deliberately sent him to Creekside Comp because they said he was 'good with his hands' and they thought he would benefit from the practical teaching there. They lived in respectable Eltham and could have sent him to Crown Woods, another of those shiny, sexy new comprehensives attended by some of his friends from primary school. Instead he was destined for Deptford, which seemed initially to him like a foreign country with its seething masses of outrageously vulgar, apparently confident boys who all seemed to know each other, thought of little but sex and football and were apparently unanimous in their support for Millwall ('Mial-wor, Mial- wor') Football Club.

Ironically, the decision turned out to be a boost to his self-esteem because, having never been top of anything before, he was amazed to be put in the A stream – a bit of happenstance which eventually enabled him to do well at school, pass A Levels, and go on to a successful career in acting and later in business. So perhaps his parents were right after all.

All this meant that Creekside Comp was effectively a secondary modern school when I joined it. Most local Deptford families just couldn't get in anywhere else. Nearly every boy in the upper streams was a grammar school reject, although many of them had plenty of ability.

But the boys ruthlessly shoved into the lower streams were, by and large, the troubled, troublesome ones conveniently forgotten by society, although they were, as the Newsom Report had called them five years earlier, 'half our future'. Even so, quite a few of them had gone to Sayers Croft in summer 1968. But some, of course, had not.

Someone had had the bright idea of merging the remaining 2E boys with their 2F counterparts – about eighteen boys in total – to create a makeshift class with a temporary timetable to cover the Sayers Croft jaunt.

Mr Baker explained all this to me in upbeat terms, as if handing over this little assembly of some of the most difficult second-year boys in the school to a naïve female with a short skirt and no teaching experience whatsoever was a triumph of progressive educational thinking.

Then Mr O'Riordan, now in charge of Lower School and practising in readiness for his new role in September, handed me a handwritten timetable for the day.

The Creekside day was chopped into eight thirty-five-minute periods, four in the morning and four in the afternoon with a break after each two. At least it was symmetrical.

My timetable for my first day gave me a double period with 2E/2F in the morning and another in the afternoon.

Of course I had nothing prepared. No one had given me any indication at all the previous week of what exactly I would be required to do when I reported for duty. I doubt that they knew themselves.

There was nothing about a subject on the timetable – just the name of the temporary group. So was I supposed to do English, which was 'my' subject with them, or should it be something else?

The only teaching I had done, after all, was three very short, quite cushy teaching practices in Chichester and Worthing – a long way from Deptford in every sense – during which everything had to be meticulously prepared and checked by a tutor. I had no idea how to think on my feet in the classroom, although it didn't take me long to learn.

'But what would you like me to do with them?' I innocently asked Mr Baker, who hadn't yet returned to the relative safety of his roost in Upper School, when Mr O'Riordan gave me the timetable sheet.

He reached casually for the nearest shelf. 'English is your subject, isn't it? Read this with them, then.' That wasn't planned either. Even at the time I knew it was simply the first thing that came into his head.

Well 'this' was a battered school-edition copy of *Shane* by Jack Schaefer. Dating from 1949, and the inspiration for a famous 1953 film, this 'western' novel remains a popular choice for teenage curriculum study in the US, but it never acquired quite the same status as a class text this side of the Atlantic.

In 1968 I had neither heard of it nor read it. 'Oh no, I can't do that,' I stammered. 'I haven't read it. I can't teach a novel I haven't read.'

What followed was my first lesson in hard-nosed Deptford cynicism – or at least in how experienced teachers used to operate to the detriment of their students, and maybe some still do. 'Oh don't worry about that, my dear,' he said, casually. 'The lads won't have read it either. You'll be fine with it.'

End of discussion. I took the weary pile of copies from the shelf and carried the books to where I'd been told the teaching room was.

These days some enlightened schools don't use bells, pips and signals because they're disruptive. At Creekside Comp, with its eight lessons, registration periods and summons to this and that, the deafening electric bell seemed to be clanging through the building, instantly stopping all thought, conversation and learning almost all the time. It also doubled up as the fire bell.

I carried my pile of books into a reasonably light and airy room – lidded desks in rows facing the front – with a playground view. The sun was shining and for a moment or two it seemed quite serene on that June day. Then the mind-numbing bell sounded the lesson change and I stood up to await 2E/F.

No one introduced me to them or them to me and I don't think they'd been told to expect me. The first I heard of them was whooping and yelling, like dervishes on speed outside the door. They were supposed to line up in the corridor and then enter the classroom, when invited, in an orderly line. That was the school rule. But of course I didn't know anything about that, so when they took advantage of me by shambling, charging or sliding into the room in twos and threes and shoving the desks round the room to suit themselves. I was already at a disadvantage.

They couldn't believe their luck, of course. They'd arrived at that door expecting one of the senior staff or, maybe, some unfortunate cover teacher pulled out of the staffroom. What they got was a twenty-one-year-old woman with flowing dark hair, knees and lower thighs on show – and quite clearly without a clue what she was doing. They may have been in the E and F stream but they weren't daft when it came to street wisdom and what's what in the world. And every one of them could spot a field day when he saw it.

Boys of this age are a very varied lot, another thing I hadn't fully appreciated until I found myself alone in a classroom with eighteen of them. Some are tiny infantile types, while others are so large, beefy and deep-voiced that they look and sound like adults. I was a bit disconcerted to find that, even at age twelve, some of these lads towered over me and I'm not particularly short. But often, as I was about to discover, it's often the 'weedy' ones who give the most bother.

And some of those larger 'lads' were definitely men, not boys. Not only were they tall, and some of them quite broad, but they had a leer in the eye when they looked at me which made me feel pretty ill-at-ease. They were mentally undressing me but hadn't reached the age when they saw any need to hide it. I could sense the naked lust.

Black boys, like black girls, tend to reach puberty earlier. There were at least two fully developed Afro-Caribbean men in that 2E/F class – although, of course, they had the minds of Year 8 boys. One of the most popular male cosmetics at that time was a range called Lynx and I think some of those men/boys poured a bottle or two over themselves every morning. Highly pungent, it mixed with the natural musky smell of boys who weren't always very clean. They were often dripping with sweat and, I suspect, other body fluids. That overpowering smell and the hormonally charged atmosphere meant that, at times, it was like being caged with a roomful of rank male tomcats who've just spotted a female.

'Start as you mean to carry on,' was the last thing my ever-helpful father had said to me that morning but inevitably I failed completely to get these gleaming-eyed lads standing behind their desks to say 'Good Morning' as we'd been made to do in my grammar school. Instead I managed, in the end, to get everyone sitting down somewhere in the room – and that was no mean achievement.

These kids were annoyed. They hadn't gone to Sayers Croft. They hadn't got their regular teachers. No one was giving them any attention. They weren't in their usual class group. The school was treating them as if they were just a nuisance – which, of course, they were.

And now they were faced with this useless young woman clutching a pile of boring, tatty books and saying repeatedly and feebly in her very un-Deptford voice, 'Oh please sit down… we're going to start this really good book today.'

I didn't even think to tell them my name. Why didn't anyone at college point out that, faced with a new class, the first thing you do is to write your name on the board?

And what on earth was I supposed to do with *Shane*? Nothing in my vacuous, project-based three years at college had indicated what you were supposed to do with a class reader – especially one you hadn't read yourself, nor even heard of until ten minutes before.

So I did the only thing I could think of which was to give out the copies and then attempt to read it round the class as we used to do when I was their age, only nine years earlier. That meant asking them to take turns in reading aloud, interspersed with me reading while they followed.

Not a good idea. I suppose it might have worked for a while with a more able group, but most of these boys had poor reading skills and reading aloud was torture. Of course they weren't going to let me humiliate them in front of each other so they subverted me and the lesson. In short they played up – with great expertise.

One large white boy kicked off. 'Have you got a boyfriend, Miss?' Another quickly chipped in with, 'Do you have sex with him?' A third called out, 'Do you use Durex?' A gravelly-voiced very dark-skinned (African?) boy started to growl obscenities under his breath, but audibly. Two Turkish boys who had deliberately placed themselves in opposite corners of the classroom shouted at each other in Turkish – obviously a practised ploy. The teamwork was generally very assured.

By the time I was walking round the room trying to shush and calm the onslaught and stop the cackles of laughter, they were all trying to outdo each other. One very small weasel-like boy viciously taunted, 'Have you got a Tampax in, Miss?'

I had no idea what to do except to pretend I hadn't heard the most offensive of these remarks, questions and comments. Instead I kept trying to refocus on *Shane* – which would have been impossible for me to sell to these kids anyway, as I knew nothing whatever about it.

And all the time I was acutely aware that I had to face them again that afternoon. Well, I reckon they thought I would probably have fled the school for ever and be holed up in a pub having the vapours by lunchtime because when I reappeared with great dread, in the afternoon, I sensed a bit of surprise, maybe even a tiny smidgeon of respect. 'Bloody hell! That silly cow has come back!'

Of course they weren't quiet or well behaved in the afternoon. They were still noisy and making deliberately inappropriate remarks but it was marginally, fractionally, better than in the morning. Perhaps they were tired.

I read them a bit of *Shane* aloud rather than asking them to read it and (sort of) held their attention for a moment or two. Then I gave out some paper and asked them to copy the drawings that the book was illustrated with – not inspired, of course, and not in the least educational but I thought, rightly as it turned out, that it would calm them down a bit if they had a task to do and be easier to manage than trying to address them and their dreadful heckling from the front.

No one at college, needless to say, had mentioned what we now call 'multiculturalism' in three whole years. My grammar school and teacher training college were both solid white. At twenty-one, apart from saying good morning to my grandparents' salt-of-the-earth West Indian neighbours and the African dentist who had treated me as a child, I don't think I had ever actually spoken to anyone of non-European ethnicity.

College didn't teach us anything about special needs either – which, of course, most of these 2E/2F boys had. My only previous experience was being taken by the college to a deeply distressing – for me, at any rate – residential institution near Billingshurst in Sussex where physically and mentally disabled 'ineducable' children were cared for.

The shameful 'ineducable' label was finally abolished in 1971 after decades of campaigning by enlightened, humane people. Then, at last, it was recognised that every child has a right to education, irrespective of disability or impairment.

But college had done nothing at all to prepare us for the 'ordinary' special needs which we would all meet and have to work with every day in mainstream schools. Hard to fathom how they could have been quite so remiss.

Well, I saw this multicultural lot with all their special needs and pubertal urges – usually twice a day – for nearly a fortnight. The truancy rate was high because, under the circumstances, and it was hard not to sympathise with them, they couldn't see much point in coming to school to be treated like tiresome leftovers while all the good stuff was going on at Sayers Croft.

Somehow I kept most of them in the room for most of the time – but education was conspicuous by its absence. And Mr O'Riordan, apparently deaf to the noise, seemed happy enough because the school's only responsibility was to have a 'teacher' in the room with them. But it was the lowest possible grade of babysitting not teaching.

I read *Shane* at home that first night so that I'd have, at least, some idea what it was about. I'm sure that if any of those boys grew up to be a keen reader he would have been put off *Shane* for life by that fortnight. And as for me, I have never opened it again and don't intend to.

Meanwhile I was also doing the odd lesson – very badly – with other classes whose teachers were at Sayers Croft or otherwise absent. No one had left any cover lessons or instructions and I had to try to find things for the boys to do. It was supply teaching at its worst. And I never knew from day to day what I'd be required to do until I arrived at school in the morning to be handed my day's timetable by Mr O'Riordan.

But the timetabling was not heavy, especially after the return of the Sayers Croft party, and I never taught more than four or five periods a day during that July. I used to take my novel with me to read in the staffroom during the slack when it was quiet and everyone else was in lessons. I was reading *Pride and Prejudice*. A case, perhaps, like that of Harold Macmillan who, during the Profumo crisis, took refuge in Jane Austen when the going got rough.

And when I wasn't doing battle with near-impossible classes or absorbed, for respite, in the doings of Elizabeth Bennett and Mr Darcy I was getting to know the staff – another steep learning curve.

At break on the first morning, for example, clutching a cup of best British Rail tea – brewed for the staff by the stalwart Mrs Polly Port who also cleared up afterwards when teachers had gone back to their classrooms – I got talking to Ray Weston.

Ray, fortyish, wore a brown store coat and smoked incessantly. Most people on the staff were smokers and indulged freely all over the building, except when they were actually in a lesson with boys. No one minded if you smoked during a non-teaching period while you marked a set of exercise books in your classroom, for example. Action on Smoking and Health (ASH) was yet another thing which wasn't going to happen for a very long time.

Woodwork was Ray's subject and, known affectionately as 'Sawdust Caesar' to the staff, he presided over a large workshop where, in his painstaking, sometimes rather laboured way, he imparted hammer and chisel skills to hundreds of boys.

It was useful, practical stuff respected by the majority of the pupils, many of whom left school well prepared to take carpentry apprenticeships. I wouldn't mind betting that there are still men working as carpenters in the Deptford area who learned their basic skills from Mr Weston.

He was a stolid, mainstream sort of guy too, unlike many of his colleagues. His wife worked as a secretary in one of the local primary schools and he had a son and daughter in their late teens.

Sadly, Ray died too young. One morning, some time after I'd left Creekside Comp, he dropped his wife at her school and stopped at the kiosk on the bridge at New Cross station to buy his cigarettes, as he did every day. Only this time he got no further. He collapsed and died in the kiosk and the first the school knew about it was when, quite uncharacteristically, he didn't show up for work and they eventually phoned Mrs Weston. I suppose his heart fell victim to all that tobacco.

But that was several years away. On my first morning at the school, Ray, puffing away as usual, made a point of coming across the staffroom to talk to me – a lone, very young, woman (Heloise wasn't around) in that mass of loud, chatty, joking men, none of whom I knew at that stage. I was completely unused to that male clubby culture and the way men – even kindly, sensitive men – josh each other all the time. It felt like a foreign country. So I was grateful for Ray's gesture. And I don't suppose he minded in the least having a chat with a buxom lass who was better looking than most of his colleagues.

He asked me about my timetable and shared a few funnies with me about some of the 'characters' in 2E and 2F. He pointed out some of the other staff too so that I began to learn a few names.

Soon we were joined by Geoff Miles, a thin, slightly bent figure in his late forties. He had oiled, slicked-down hair, very thick bottle glasses and an outrageous, rapier-like line in witty observations.

Geoff, who taught science, was to become by far my closest friend in the school and remained a family friend until his death in 2008.

He befriended me in every way he could, almost from day one. Nick has always said that Geoff took a shine to me because he 'fancied' me and yes, that's true. I was always aware of it but it wasn't mutual. I liked him, admired him and enjoyed his company, but I was engaged to, and very much in love with, a man my own age and didn't have any sexual feelings at all for Geoff. Anyway I could only ever have been a well-maybe-under-other-circumstances fantasy for him. He had a wife he was devoted to and to whom I was soon introduced – and two teenage children I saw occasionally while they were still living at home. For his daughter and son, I was a family joke, although I didn't realise that until I called him one evening only to hear his daughter yell, 'Dad, it's your girlfriend on the phone.'

One way and another Geoff and I spent a great deal of time together over the years but, although he talked bluntly and often outrageously about sex, nothing of a sexual nature ever passed between us – although I'm pretty sure there were people on the Creekside Comp staff who later came to suspect otherwise. He and I were an unusual alliance and we raised eyebrows amongst our colleagues, as well as an amused daughterly eyebrow in his own home.

One of the things Geoff asked me, when we first met, was where I lived. When I told him about my awkward journey he offered to pick me up at a point about half a mile from my parents' home that he passed each morning on the way to Deptford from Beckenham where he lived. That was a real help. And the in-car chats were one of the reasons that I got to know Geoff so well.

Geoff, about the same age as my father, had been prevented from active wartime service by his very poor eyesight. Instead he had 'idled for four years' in the Civil Service before, like my father, signing up for post-war teacher training.

Although it was very hard to persuade Geoff to be serious about anything for more than about two minutes, I did once coax out of him the admission that he wanted to 'do something useful'. He could never, he told me, be anything 'like a bookmaker' – the very word spat out with contempt. And he'd been teaching in Deptford – most of the time with, or under, Harry Baker –

since 1946. He had, in fact, started there before I was born, which amused me.

Geoff's politics were well to the left of Karl Marx and his rational atheism was very assertive, especially if you mentioned Catholics. 'Take the bodily assumption of the Virgin Mary,' he'd say chirpily. 'They don't mean anything metaphysical, you know. They're talking about fourteen stone of Jewess rising spontaneously off the ground and disappearing into the clouds.' I never quite understood why he was so convinced that the BVM was obese. He would then add, 'And never trust a Catholic either. However friendly they seem, they're taught from babyhood to have no truck with heretics – and they mean you and me.'

When I first met Geoff he was so opposed to capitalism and usury that he refused to deposit money in interest-bearing accounts. He mellowed a bit on that later when he inherited quite a lot of money from his father and from his in-laws.

Mean with himself but generous with others, he remains the only person I've ever known who would dry coffee grounds on paper on the windowsill to get a second use out of them.

He was also a Heath Robinson-type eccentric. Not for him, and the long-suffering Coral, his wife, anything as expensive as an electric blanket or even as ordinary as a hot water bottle. With his usual impish seriousness he explained to me that he'd rigged up an arrangement with an electric light bulb screwed into the inside of an old warming pan to pre-heat their bed.

A classical music buff who played piano and flute a bit, Geoff was also an enthusiastic photographer and collector of cameras, an avid reader, no mean cook, keen on quirky antiques and good at DIY car maintenance – quite a polymath. But he had no time for pompousness, priests, hypocrites or Conservative Party supporters.

In school Geoff was legendary and by far the strongest personality on the staff. To hear him berating some hapless boy in the corridor was a masterclass in verbal fluency. The crosser and louder Geoff got the more complex and articulate was the invective.

In his classes he got on well with the boys because underneath all the bluff he liked them and, although he didn't have a shred of sentimentality, was dedicated to doing his best for them. He taught thousands of boys a lot of science and knew, usually without being confrontational, exactly how to tame the apparently untameable.

Quietly, most of them thought the world of Mr Miles, although he'd have brushed that off with one of his flippant witticisms if you'd pointed it out. When he drove me round the back streets of Deptford on the way to and from school, many a swarthy, shifty, suspicious-looking youth or man, former pupils I presumed, would wave to him cheerfully. 'See – I know every villain in the district,' he'd say happily. 'If I ever need to disappear underground I'll have no problems.'

In 1968 Geoff held no official management post. He'd always turned them down because he didn't want to 'join the enemy'. But every staffroom has an unappointed, unofficial lead teacher – an alpha male as it were – who dominates the dynamic and whom everyone respects and listens to. At Creekside Comp Geoff was definitely the one.

CHAPTER THREE

As those pre-summer holiday weeks wore on, colleagues went on eyeing me up. Testosterone ruled the staffroom just as firmly as it did the Creekside classrooms and playground. Some men seemed to have a fixation with my legs and knees. Others would pretend not to be looking at me but I'd catch them stealing sideways glances. Tights were not the norm in 1968 and I was still wearing traditional stockings and suspenders under my shortish skirts – the sort of thing which drives a certain sort of man wild, although I didn't fully understand that at the time.

In the end it was Geoff – who else – who warned me that I needed to be a bit more careful about how I sat in the staffroom. 'You've got one or two of the men salivating at the sight of you, girl,' he said, adding in his usual forthright, half jokey way, 'They'll be trying to finger your fanny next.'

Point taken. I started experimenting with newfangled tights, which I never really found comfortable. The crotch gets nearer to your knees every time you need to adjust them – or at least it did then.

Gradually I got to know more staff, some by talking to them, others from observation. And it was something of an eye opener because at least half were, clearly, very clearly, in the wrong job. Not only could they not resist fantasising about the twenty-one-year-old 'girl' in their midst, they were lousy teachers too.

Pete Sargeant, for example, was a gruff, angry, loud-voiced man in his forties. He taught brickwork and in all the years I knew him I never saw him smile. He was perpetually either berating boys angrily or talking angrily about them to anyone who was silly enough to get caught and have to listen. Either way the anger was a constant.

He had an apparently quite serious disability and walked with two sticks. Inevitably he gestured with his sticks as he talked and often prodded, or worse, boys with them. He reminded me of one of those Shakespearean characters like Richard III, flawed in personality as well as in body. Of course, he was a man most people gave a wide berth to.

The most extraordinary thing about him, though, was his home life although, perhaps, it explained a lot. Maybe he was so cowed at home that he got it out of his system by being surly in school.

His father-in-law was a provincial bishop – a fact Pete would make sure you knew in the first ten seconds of any conversation with him. And it was definitely true. We knew the Bishop's name and it was easily checkable. Geoff had done it long since. And I soon confirmed it for myself in Crockford's when I had an idle moment in the public library.

The Bishop's daughter – I always imagined her as being like Trollope's Mrs Proudie, although I never met her – had borne him two children. 'Pete engaging with a woman for long enough to engender two children! Some things really do challenge the imagination!' was Geoff's view.

There was nothing remotely refined or cultured about Pete. He showed no sign of religion either. How on earth did he ever meet a bishop's daughter unless, in youth, he was employed to re-point the palace walls? And what, pray, did she see in him, one of the least attractive men I've ever come across? Well, maybe she liked 'a bit of rough' or had reached a certain age and saw Pete as her only chance. If so she must have been unimaginably desperate. Perhaps she was pregnant and forced by an irate bishop to spend the rest of her life with a man that no one could possibly have found sexy except briefly on a very dark night, if you'd had a great deal to drink and had never before been allowed out of parental control.

It would have been pointless to ask him how he'd met his beloved – although he'd have been delighted to tell you – because he was unreliable. There were, for example, at least a dozen stories going around school about how he'd become disabled.

Like many inadequate teachers with personality problems he loved to harangue captive pupils with his stories. The boys were probably the only audience he ever got. It meant that they could regale these versions – a different one for each group. Some explanations were implausibly romantic, such as Pete's having been pinned down by a falling beam in a burning building while trying to rescue a child or a beautiful woman, or having nearly drowned on a sinking ship but miraculously escaping with just his leg injury. In a different mood he'd tell you he'd been injured by crashing his motorbike or falling off a roof. Since he was a brickie, the latter is probably the most likely.

At Creekside Comp Pete had a large brickwork workshop on the ground floor just inside the door near the stinking bogs. It also had a door onto the playground so that he could park his elderly estate car very close and didn't have far to walk. I once moved his car across the playground for him when he couldn't, for some reason, get it close enough. The inside of the vehicle was a bit like him – untidy, angry and unappealing.

I often wonder, looking back, just how severe the disability was or whether he'd developed it as a part of his always furious personality. There was no lift in the building but he was able to get himself up a flight of stairs to the staffroom at break times, so the disability was evidently manageable.

I suppose the boys learned some brickwork from 'Old Sargeant' but no one liked him. He was too unpredictable and volatile and, anyway, they knew he was a liar. And kids loathe that.

Another man on the staff who should definitely have been doing something else was amiable, impervious, incompetent Timmy Fletcher.

Short, bespectacled and fortyish, Timmy taught music – except that he didn't. Ever. Music was not exactly respected in the school and Timmy was the sole proponent. That meant that at some point in the week he was timetabled to teach each of the eighteen or so classes in Lower School, some of them twice.

Usually the last person in the staffroom at the end of break, he would, eventually, bumble along the corridor, often talking to himself cheerfully, towards his teaching room where the boys would be running amok.

One of the class would have been on the lookout for Sir for at least five minutes. When he told the others that Timmy was approaching the entire class would roar as loudly as they knew how. You could hear it all over the building. Everyone knew when Timmy had arrived at his lesson.

The racket – which had nothing to do with music – continued all the time that Timmy was in the room, although it was slightly less disruptive for the rest of us once he'd shut the door. He was one of those rare teachers whose classes were less controlled when he was there than when he wasn't – a dubious distinction. In short, the boys would probably have been quieter, and learned more, if Timmy hadn't bothered to turn up at the lesson at all.

Once in the classroom he would play the piano and invite the boys to sing from hymn books or other song books – or play records. No one took any notice of him and the boys simply continued to whoop and yell around him. One of his teaching strategies was to thrash dangerously and sadistically round the classroom with a cane in a feeble effort to get the boys to sing.

He coped with his abject failure as a teacher by retreating into denial. He remained ebullient, never took time off school, which was more than could be said for many of his colleagues, and simply seemed to have convinced himself that his 'teaching' was normal.

It was all rather a shame because Timmy was a good musician. He'd been a bandsman in the war and was a very reasonable pianist. He would play hymns in assembly, sung, of course, by no one except staff, and then treat us to a bit of Chopin or Liszt as we left. On one occasion he casually pulled a violin out of a case and sat in the corner of the staffroom quietly playing part of the Tchaikovsky violin concerto softly to himself in the same way as someone else, with five minutes to spare, might open a book or glance at a newspaper. It was so unassuming that I doubt most of the staff present even noticed. Definitely the wrong man in the wrong job.

Geoff said (there wasn't much he didn't know about his colleagues) that there was a Mrs Fletcher at home with whom Timmy lived in unspeaking hostility. For many years his home life had, apparently, been a miserable and lonely world of separate rooms, silent meals and 'Tell your father to pay the electricity bill.'

Then there was the glittering Pat McGuire, a brilliant – or he should have been – young history teacher of ambiguous sexuality. Pat had a good degree from Trinity College Dublin and my first question should have been, 'Why is a man with a brain like that languishing at Creekside Comp?' But it wasn't. I was still taking things at face value.

The answer to the question I didn't ask was drink. Pat drank – and drank and drank. He was tall and quite fine looking, with intelligent eyes behind glasses. He was also very entertaining to talk to with his rich Irish voice, a fund of stories and forthright views. On a good day he was an outstanding teacher, well able to enthral every boy in every class. Sadly the good days were few and far between.

He would often sway into school clearly still drunk from a binge the previous night, unshaven and unkempt. Sometimes we suspected he hadn't been home or been to bed. His clothes were shiny with lack of care. 'Why are you wearing the lining rather than the suit, Pat?' Geoff asked him one day with that characteristic witty rudeness that only he could get away with.

When he was in that state Pat couldn't be bothered to enthral his classes, and the boys more or less did as they pleased.

He also coached rugby. Years later one of the boys who started at Creekside in the same year as I did told me that Pat was wont to invite his sixth-form rugby lads back to his flat for drunken brawls after matches. On one occasion he said, 'Come on, let's all get our penises out to compare.' No one did except Pat. In the end one of the more mature and quick-thinking boys managed to defuse the situation by saying, 'OK, Pat, that's enough. Put it away now. Enough's enough, old chap.'

But more often than not – once a week at least – he wouldn't turn up at all and whatever excuse he'd muttered about flu or a stomach upset when, or if – he didn't always bother – he phoned in, we all knew that he was just too badly hung-over to make the effort. Like everyone else at Creekside Comp I quickly got to know Pat's timetable because I was so often sent to babysit his teacherless classes in my very inadequate way.

Pat had been on the staff for some time when I joined and it was quite a while before he eventually disappeared. Incredible by today's standards that he was tolerated for even a week. The same boy who described the penis incident told me that in the early 1990s, he and a friend were buttonholed by a shabby, homeless man in a central London pub – it turned out to be Pat McGuire who'd recognised a former pupil and spotted what he hoped was an opportunity for a free drink or two.

Creekside Comp had been cobbled together a few years before I arrived there through a series of mergers – which is probably why there was nothing very unified about it and its two buildings on opposite sides of Deptford.

Mr Baker was inclined, in his grand-old-man, Mr Chips-ian manner, to tell newcomers like me that he'd been in the same school all his teaching life and had risen through the ranks there to headship.

No, no, according to Geoff, who'd also been around a long time and regarded Baker as a useless old bumbler, this was not exactly true. Baker began, when he was twenty-one, in one of the schools and eventually got the headship of the comp towards the end of his career. But there were plenty of long-servers on the staff, Geoff amongst them, who had taught in one of the other component schools. Then they, and their school, had been absorbed into this final, rather disparate (and desperate?) merger. Baker and his hands-off ways were relatively new to them.

One of the schools which had been merged – more than once, I think – was an old 'technical' school, the influence of which was still a strong presence in 1968.

Technical schools were formed after the 1944 Education Act and lasted until the late 1950s. They were meant to offer a craft-based education to young people, mostly boys, with practical aptitude. In practice only a few opened and they were short-lived – like the one in Deptford which had been merged.

Its legacy, though, was a strong focus on practical building crafts for the boys at Creekside Comp – probably the school's only real strength.

The row of craft workshops in the playground included plumbing, plastering and metalwork facilities, while Pete Sargeant's brick empire and Ray Weston's woodwork shop were inside the building. These facilities were staffed either by men like Ray who had taught in the old technical school or by part-timers who also worked at the local further education college with which the school had what would now be called a 'strong link' or perhaps even 'a partnership'.

One such man was Mike Churchill who taught plumbing for three quarters of the week at Creekside Comp and spent a small amount of time at the college.

Eyes glinting, Mike buttonholed me for staffroom conversation very early on. And still taking things at face value I didn't spot the danger. In my innocence, and out of politeness, I asked him what he taught. Well, I was genuinely quite interested because, given my girls' grammar school background, the whole notion of plumbing as a school curriculum subject seemed exotically other-worldly. So when he invited me to see his workshop for myself after break that morning when neither of us was teaching, I accepted with alacrity.

Mike was probably twice my age and it simply never occurred to me that he was thinking about anything except plumbing and being kind to a woman young enough to be his daughter. Actually, of course, to use a nasty twenty-first-century expression, he was 'grooming' me.

I duly went to the plumbing workshop where he showed me the boys' work and explained what sort of assignments he did with them – all the time moving in uncomfortably close to me and glancing rather too often at my legs. I was quite glad to get away, although didn't think a great deal of it until lunchtime when I casually told Geoff that I'd visited Mike Churchill in his workshop.

'Oh bugger!' he said, quite seriously by his standards. 'Mike didn't entice you into that metallic lair of his, did he? Are you OK?' It was enough. I made sure I was never alone with Mike again.

Much later, I discovered that Mike was Heloise's landlord and given to calling on her when her husband was out. His usual purpose was to propose the granting of sexual favours in lieu of rent arrears. I don't think he ever got his way but she was deeply frightened of him. Geoff, who knew everything, was well aware of all this, of course. Hence his concern at my interchange with Mike – not a man, I suspect, who would stay in school employment these days for very long, although he wasn't a bad plumbing teacher.

Not all staff were angry, incompetent or lecherous though.

Jack Rowlands was in charge of English in Lower School. And, come the new term, he would also be Deputy Head of Lower School when Mr O'Riordan took over as Head.

Jack was articulate, funny, ambitious, balding and thirty-something. When I first met him he had almost completed an external degree in economics at Goldsmiths College – all part of his career plan towards headship.

He did eventually achieve his ambition, having marched ruthlessly, as really ambitious people always do, over many people and shed a wife or two en route.

He drove a Triumph Herald – a stylish but determined car like its owner – extremely well and was, at the time, the only person I'd ever met to hold the Institute of Advanced Motorists' qualification.

Jack had much more idea about how to nurture a new teacher than most of his colleagues and thought that some of my spare time could usefully be spent on a bit of what would now be called 'induction'. What he really meant was would I like to sit in on one of his lessons to see how it's done?

And so it was that a day or two later I was sitting in on a surprisingly 'progressive' lesson. Jack had the boys sitting seminar-style round a 'table' consisting of desks pushed together in a block. This was so that they could discuss the passage he was presenting. He was using a text about cars from *English Through Experience Book III* by A. W. Rowe and Peter Emens. I still have a copy of it. Jack was by far the most gifted teacher I had ever seen in action and, actually, to this day he'd still be in my top five.

I watched and listened incredulously as he led the boys through the information about the new (1963) specifications for the Ford Consul Cortina and Hillman Minx Deluxe. He coaxed and questioned. He made sure every boy in the group was involved. He adeptly explained to them and, incidentally, to me that the CC rating in a car refers to the volume of cylinder swept by the pistons.

The whole lesson, at the end of which he sent the boys off to do some related written work for homework, was fascinating, both in terms of content and method. I'd never imagined, for example, that an English lesson could go beyond 'literature' and the mechanics of using language correctly. It taught me more about English teaching than three years at college had done.

I learned a lot from Jack's deceptively laid-back manner too. He was assertive and firm but friendly. No boy was in any doubt of the expected standard of behaviour. In effect he treated them like responsible young adults and not once did he put anyone down.

Jack also sent me off to watch another younger colleague in action with a first-year group. He was impressive too. He had

English Through Experience Book I and, with enviable control, had them throwing paper aeroplanes round the room and writing about flight.

Slowly we limped on towards the end of term and the summer holiday. When it was difficult, as it often was, I told myself that all would be different in the new term when I would have my own regular classes.

'You'll all have your timetables for September at least a week before we break up so that you can plan and prepare,' Mr O'Riordan said several times.

'You won't,' said Geoff. 'They say it every year, but we never get a timetable until the first day back.' Of course he was right and I left for the summer holiday without a clue what would be required of me in the new term.

Summer 1968 – with the invasion of newly liberalised Czechoslovakia by Russia with troops and tanks about to shake us all on 21 August – stretched ahead. I was at work for most of it.

During my three years at college I had worked each holiday at an ILEA play centre back at home in South London. ILEA ran these centres, amazingly by today's standards, as a free service. One was open in each area after school during term time so that the children had somewhere to go until their parents finished work.

During the holidays the demand was much greater, so they expanded the provision by opening some other schools all day. Regular play centre staff ran craft, sport and singing game activities, but they needed extra help to cope with holiday numbers. Hence the employment of students like me.

Summer 1968 was the last time I did it because, truth to tell, I found it pretty boring. If you weren't assigned something specific to do a lot of it was merely standing about watching the children. Like playground duty for hours at a stretch.

During summer 1968, knowing that I'd already earned some money supply teaching, I decided I could afford to do afternoons only at the play centre – this time on the Honor Oak Estate –

rather than all day. That meant I could concentrate on driving lessons in the morning, have a bit of time to myself and be fresh to spend every evening with Nick – which was what I really wanted to do most, of course.

In the last week of the summer holiday Nick and I hired a canal boat with another couple we'd known as long as we'd known each other. She had been at primary school with me and he was at secondary school with Nick. Puttering our way from Rugby to Llangollen was a good final wind-down before the start of my first term as a fully-fledged, or at least 'probationary', teacher.

CHAPTER FOUR

I've always liked September. It's the season of new pencils, exercise books and uniform. From age five until I left school and then on through all the years I worked as a teacher, I enjoyed the sense of the fresh new school year which comes in September, counterpointed with autumnal sunshine, shortening days, chilly mornings, conkers and Michaelmas daisies.

So it wasn't 'unwillingly to school' for me in September 1968. I felt pretty buoyed up and bright-eyed as I walked up the road to wait for Geoff at our agreed meeting point.

Soon he appeared in his elderly but reliable, home-maintained, brown Morris Traveller complete with that businesslike and distinctive wooden framework and doors at the back. Geoff and his car were yet more evidence to support my theory that, as with dogs, people grow to resemble their cars. Or, at least, that they choose cars which reflect their personality.

'The timetable will be a pig's breakfast and half the staff will be absent,' he said with his customary prescience. 'You and I are just the bloody infantry,' he continued cheerily as we progressed through Brockley towards the increasingly industrial descent into Deptford, past Robinson's Flour Mill and the huge blocks of 1930s council flats which lined the road leading to the school.

Robinson's Flour Mill stood majestically on the corner of Deptford Church Street and Deptford Broadway where a newish building belonging to Lewisham College now stands next to the Docklands Light Railway. The old mill burned down one night during the time I worked in Deptford. They brought more than a hundred fire engines from all over London and you could see the pall of smoke for miles around. Arson, of course, and Geoff and I were sure we must know the perpetrators – or at least their younger brothers in my case – although, as far as I know, no one was ever charged.

But on that first morning Robinsons was still milling flour in its usual smelly way as we drove past en route for the new term.

Many schools, even then, would have started the term with some sort of planning, reorientation event such as a staff meeting. Not so Creekside Comp. We arrived – Geoff and I usually got there quite early – in time for a bit of what-have-you-been-up-to-since-July-type chat with colleagues as, one by one, they appeared in the ever-smoky staffroom. And across the corridor we could hear phones ringing and being answered by Janet and Margaret. People were already phoning, I later realised, to announce that for whatever reason they would not be gracing Creekside Comp with their presence that day.

Then Mr O'Riordan turned up, a bit half-hearted and oddly unassertive in manner. He muttered a few greetings to the people nearest to him and spread out the timetables on a side table. I was to be, I learned, form teacher to class 1B so I needed my timetable as well as theirs.

We wouldn't actually put these timetables into operation until after break. The first job was to get down to the yard to collect form 1B and take them to Room 9. Next there'd be an assembly and then I had to give 1B their timetable and explain to them everything they needed to know about this school, about which I knew so little.

Since then, I've always argued that it is never a good idea to put new staff in charge of new pupils because neither can help the other. Putting the blind in charge of the blind is usually a recipe for disaster. But actually 1B and I fell in love with each other almost at sight and, quite quickly, we became a team.

On that first morning I went down to the yard with the rest of the staff where hundreds of second and third years were charging about, kicking footballs and yelling. In stark contrast, 200 or so mostly well-scrubbed, new first years in their blazers and dark trousers were standing about looking wary, ill-at-ease, apprehensive, terrified or, in a few cases, cocky in a vain attempt to cover what they were really feeling. None of them, until their names were barked out sergeant-majorishly, even knew what forms they were going into.

Ian Castle, a delightful, caring professional man with easy authority, blew a whistle and read out the lists so that the first-year boys could line up in forms. It was at that stage that the boys discovered whether they were destined for 1A or 1G and I know the decisions took some of them by surprise.

Like so many of my new colleagues, Ian came from a craft background. A career signwriter he had taught at the local FE college before moving full-time to Creekside Comp where he taught art and maths. He was still moonlighting, and augmenting his income as a part-time signwriter when I knew him. He told me, for example, about a job he'd recently done for Coutts Bank. Puzzled about their continued non-payment of his invoice he sent them a reminder only to be told that Coutts, at that time, settled their accounts just once a year. Ian was crossly fascinated by what that policy said about the craftspeople Coutts usually employed if they were prepared to put up with waiting up to twelve months for their dues. Not to mention Coutts's disdainful, superior attitude.

Ian's job at Creekside Comp included liaising with local primary schools and doing a bit of pastoral work with first-year boys as they settled in. He did this with kindness and aplomb and was universally liked and respected.

Ian was form teacher to class 1A in parallel with 'my' 1B and I taught both classes for English. One way and another Ian and I had to work together quite closely and I learned a lot from him. His wife was training to be a teacher when I first met him and they had two primary school age daughters. On the first morning of term, Ian lined up the classes and made sure that the right form teacher was with each of them. Then we marched them into the building.

1B and I were assigned to Room 9, on the bottom corridor, just along from the terrible toilets and Pete Sargeant's cheerless brickwork shop. It was a darkish room because of the protective grilles on the outside which kept the glass safe from stray footballs in the playground. Nonetheless it was mine – my very first classroom – and I felt like a queen in a palace. It wasn't quite what Virginia Woolf meant by 'a room of one's own' but it certainly came close.

That feeling did not, however, last because – inevitably – there was a fly in the Creekside ointment. There was I thinking how lucky I was to have this nice room with its neat rows of pupil desks and a big desk at the front for me, from which I could preside magisterially.

But no one told me about the coal lorry.

The school had pretty efficient solid fuel heating which meant that it guzzled many tons of coal. And it had to be delivered. Frequently. The cellars, I soon discovered, lay below Room 9 and the coal chute was immediately outside the window about three feet from my desk.

The first time we had a delivery – on the second or third day of term – the room suddenly went darker than ever because almost all the light was instantly blocked by the coal lorry. As the coal was forcibly shot down the chute the whole room vibrated. The juddering, bone-rattling noise made it impossible to speak or even think. I've never been in an earthquake but I found out how it would feel – fast and frequently.

This Blitz-like experience took me by surprise on the first occasion because I had no idea what it was. Each delivery took half an hour or so and happened twice a week in winter. No wonder no one wanted Room 9 and it had been foisted on an unknowing newcomer so readily. I soon learned to adapt what we were doing in the classroom as soon as I saw the coal lorry so that no one needed to speak.

There was another problem with that room too. 1968/9 was the winter during which an almost forgotten national experiment was tried. We didn't put the clocks back in October and ran on British Standard Time right through the winter. It meant, when the days were at their shortest, leaving home in pitch darkness. Then came the less than glamorous experience of dawn over Deptford at about 9am. Room 9 was so dark from November to February that we needed all the lights on most of the time. I felt like a mother mole in charge of thirty-five mole-lets or whatever young moles are called.

By the end of my first year I had learned a few ropes and become more assertive. I complained bitterly about Room 9 and was, for my second year, given a much nicer light and airy room on the top floor, which seemed like a different world.

But that was later. For the moment there I was in Room 9 with 1B on Day One. First job: call and mark the register, which had been neatly created by Janet or Margaret in a standard, foolscap, green-covered, ILEA standard issue, gridded booklet.

That was a first too because no one had ever made me do this very basic teacherly task on teaching practice. And because the school day was traditionally divided into two separate sessions the register had to be called morning and afternoon. I quickly grew very adept at putting in those alternating obliques in blue or black ink to indicate boys present and nice round zeros in red for the absences. It created a pleasing, rather satisfying pattern.

This was a fresh start for both the boys and me so I told them firmly that each boy had to reply 'Yes, Miss Hillyer' when I called his name – once, that is, I had learned how to pronounce their names, including the one with a vowel-free Polish surname and the tricky appellations of one or two Asian boys.

There were several boys of what we would now call Afro-

Caribbean ancestry too but their names were mostly Anglicised, easy to say and easy to spell. One for example was named 'Cookson' and another 'Blair' – an echo, I suppose, of the nineteenth-century British slave owners whose names had been imposed on these boys' ancestors.

Register done, it was off to assembly in the dingy, first-floor hall. The one above it on the second floor was much lighter and pleasanter but for some reason we never held assemblies there.

I already knew what a stark and dispiriting business assembly was at Creekside Comp, having attended them for weeks the previous term. There were no chairs. Boys stood in sullen rows with teachers at the side glaring at them. It must have been quite a culture shock for 1B and the rest of the first year, fresh from their warm, friendly primary schools.

Tatty hymn sheets were passed along the rows and then we all pretended to sing 'Eternal Father Strong to Save' or 'When a Knight Won His Spurs' or 'Praise My Soul the King of Heaven' while Timmy Fletcher played the piano – the only thing he was any good at.

Jim O'Riordan stood on the stage at the front and gazed balefully at the assembled boys over his hymn sheet. Then he threw a few incomprehensible prayers at them before leading a mumbled, embarrassed recitation of the Lord's Prayer.

Then came the notices, orders and injunctions. In practice it was usually a very off-putting, often very stern, lecture on what not to do. Strong on the negatives and very light on positives.

And I once saw Mr O'Riordan bash a boy in the front row on the head with a bible because the hapless child – he must have been a first year or he wouldn't have been at the front – wasn't paying attention.

The bible, an unconsciously ironic weapon, was what happened to be in the teacher's hand because we were in assembly – the daily act of corporate worship required by the 1944 Education Act. It was a literal case of 'bible bashing'. There was nothing much to stop such an action because corporal punishment was still legal and, in various forms, used all the time at Creekside Comp. Jack Rowlands was, for example, remarkably free with the cane for a man so enlightened in other ways. He thought nothing of caning a boy for tipping his chair backwards in class, for instance.

After this less than uplifting experience of assembly, 1B and I returned to Room 9 where we had just over an hour to acquaint ourselves with what we had to do – the vagaries of the timetable – and to start to get to know each other.

Meanwhile the real drama of the day was going on in the Head's office, although I didn't hear about it until break.

Mr O'Riordan was, I realised that day, a man with problems, although I never quite got to the bottom of what they were. On the first morning in his new job he had what the French call a *crise de nerfs* or, as Jack Rowlands put it with casual irreverence in the staffroom at break: 'O'Riordan just blew up.'

I suppose Jim must have had some sort of hysterical attack – weeping, raging, headbanging or something. Whatever the exact symptoms of his sudden-onset mental illness were, he went, or was sent, home before lunch on the first day of term.

Thereafter he only ever appeared at school for two or three days before succumbing again to his illness, He was effectively absent for the whole of that school year and most of the next before leaving to take up a low-level teaching post in another school.

Jim was a staunch Roman Catholic of Irish ancestry. He had eight children ranging in age from thirtyish down to a toddler. The first four had been born to him and his first wife who had then died. When I encountered Jim he was married to another teacher, a much younger woman, with whom he had had four more, quite young, children.

He was, by all accounts, a fine maths teacher and many of his colleagues spoke highly of him, but of course I saw none of that. The man I didn't really know at all was merely an absentee head with whom the staff soon became increasingly irritated.

Jim didn't drive and Geoff offered to pick him up because Jim lived close to our usual route. Occasionally we transported him but far more often we waited five or ten minutes and then went to school without him when Jim didn't show up.

Geoff, always decent at heart, was – I think – trying to help. He had worked with Jim for a long time and was well aware of Jim's better qualities. On the other hand, Jim's Catholicism and the consequent large family was something of a stumbling block and Geoff had, in the privacy of his car with me, been pretty scathing about his colleague.

On one occasion, Geoff and I called – by arrangement – on Jim and his wife for a cup of tea on the way home after school. None of this was altruism on Geoff's part. More an attempt, as he saw it, to persuade Jim to toe the line. We found him looking relaxed and content with a couple of his youngest children in tow in his front room, for all the world as if he were on holiday.

I didn't know enough about mental illness to make a judgement so I just spoke when I was spoken too, drank my tea, kept my eyes and ears open and exchanged pleasantries with Jim's wife. Geoff, who wasn't renowned for his tolerance, and didn't have much truck with mental illness anyway, was convinced Jim was malingering. And our visit to the family home did nothing to persuade him otherwise.

On the first day of term, Jim's 'eruption' – or whatever it was – and subsequent disappearance left Jack Rowlands suddenly, and quite unexpectedly, in charge of Lower School.

On the second morning Jack came to school as usual but within an hour or two he was running a high temperature, coughing and suffering a severe headache. So he had to go home too because he obviously had a nasty dose of flu.

So for the rest of that week, until Jack returned to work the following Monday, Tim Ellis was in charge. Tim was still in his twenties, a tough nut, an old boy of the school and pretty good at his job, but I think he was a bit surprised to get this headship thrust upon him so suddenly – even for a few days.

At home on the Tuesday evening I recounted incredulously this sorry tale of headmasters going down like dominoes. 'Well, at this rate, you'll be in charge by the end of the week!' quipped my father.

Fortunately it didn't come to that because I had the challenge of bonding with 1B to deal with. And what a delight they were: innocent, keen, anxious and desperate to make a good impression on each other and on me and to make a worthwhile start in their new school – although it certainly wouldn't have been a first choice for most of them. In fact I doubt that the majority of them had Creekside Comp on the family list of possible schools at all. They had simply been assigned to it as the last possible resort.

When children transfer to secondary school many of them are just that. They have yet to acquire teenage cynicism and hormones. When I met my first class almost everyone in 1B was still a little boy.

Most of them seemed to be called Mark, Gary or Stephen. I refused from the outset to call them by their surnames as if they were army recruits or prisoners, although the entire complement of male teachers in the school routinely did.

Take Mark Shaw, a fresh-faced boy with thick erratic ginger hair which bounced up and down as he walked. He lived in Brockley a few doors from Nick and his parents. So my soon-to-be mother-in-law knew Mrs Shaw by sight and now got into the habit of chatting to her once it was realised that Mark was in my class.

South London is, and was, like a village. So it isn't that surprising that Mr Shaw, a piano tuner, and my father soon realised they knew each other too. They exercised their dogs in the same park late each evening and passed the time of day together while throwing sticks and balls for their respective canines.

Mark was enthusiastic but troubled. He was reasonably bright and, by personality, a 'grammar school type'. He was verbally confident and didn't speak with a Deptford, or even South London, accent. He loved cricket and didn't mind saying so, which made him a potential misfit in the football-sodden culture of Deptford where most boys aggressively supported Millwall and thought of little else.

Mark had failed his eleven plus and hadn't managed to get into any of the better comprehensive schools at the end of the borough where he (and I) lived. This must have been particularly difficult for him because his brother and only sibling, who was ten years older, had been through grammar school and – he must have been about the same age as me – was already working as a young teacher.

Mark with his unusual interests, bouncy walk, relatively refined voice and rather adult manner was exactly the sort who could very easily have been bullied at Creekside Comp. In fact he worked hard, found friends who were – like him – very much their own people. Years later Mark managed to pass some A Levels and follow his brother into teaching.

When I met him in the street, by chance, in the mid-1980s he told me that 1B and I had 'saved' him from the demoralised fate which seemed to await most eleven plus failures. We'd made him feel valued and worthwhile again – which was lovely for me to hear all those years later.

Then there was Khalid Verjee. He and his family had been evicted from Kenya with many thousands of other Asians only a few months earlier, in the same way that in the early seventies Idi Amin threw large numbers of businessmen and other Asians out of Uganda virtually with only the clothes they were wearing. The governments of both countries, meanwhile, simply appropriated – or stole – the businesses, homes, cars and other possessions belonging to these hardworking Asians.

Khalid, a smiling, willing, but evidently traumatised refugee, had attended a Deptford primary school for one term. Although English is the official language of Kenya, he had clearly not been taught by (British) native speakers and his oral expression was very quaint and distinctly un-Deptfordian. He had no concept of chatting informally to a teacher – as, say, Mark Shaw had in his urbane way. Khalid was used to much more distant, authoritarian teachers and it showed in his deferential manner.

The eviction of the Kenyan Asians, and the accommodation of so many of these penniless refugees in Britain, because Kenya is a former colony, had been in the news for months. It felt very strange to me to have a living, breathing example of it in my classroom. Until then the whole African Asian 'problem' had seemed rather academic and remote. It was as if current affairs were coming to life before my eyes.

Wonderfully named Bartholomew Paradise was part of a large Jamaican family who lived in the flats in nearby Tidemill Road. He was delightful – courteous, friendly and conscientious. Diligent and bright, he got on very well with his classmates, always had a smile for me and plenty of sensible things to say in class discussions.

But he never came to school on Monday mornings, which puzzled me for several weeks. Casual – and strangely regular – truancy just didn't seem to fit in with the rest of his personality. His parents were salt-of-the-earth, evangelical Christians and his older brothers were all spoken highly of by staff at Creekside Comp who remembered them. Bartholomew was the youngest in the family and I suspect he was also the most intelligent.

In the end, I tackled him gently about those missing Monday mornings. He looked a bit troubled. 'Well, Miss,' he said, 'I come to school as soon as I can but it depends what time the rent man comes and sometimes he's late.'

The Paradise family, it transpired, paid their rent weekly, in cash and on the nail. This was long before the days of automatic bank transfers and I doubt that they had a bank account anyway. All Bartholomew's family worked hard and long hours, including his mother who, along with his father and elder siblings, would have been paid in cash on Friday evenings. For this family getting into debt or owing money would have been unthinkable.

So when the rent man made his regular Monday morning call, as far as Mr and Mrs Paradise were concerned, someone had to be there to hand over the money. And because everyone else was at work, the job fell to Bartholomew.

Yes, the Paradise family valued education, but nothing was more important than paying the rent. It was a situation totally unlike anything I'd ever experienced with my grammar school friends, in my own family or social circle but how could I argue? Of course, they were technically breaking the law. It was 'condoned truancy' after all. But their motives were so inarguably laudable that I turned a blind eye, as did the school's Education Welfare Officer when I explained the situation. Anyway Bartholomew worked so hard and sensibly at school for the rest of the time that he never fell behind.

Stephen Marconi was a tall slim fresh-faced boy with lots of friends from primary school. He was friendly, forthcoming and apparently happy to chat cheerfully to me about anything and everything – as he had with his primary teacher – except, I soon realised, about one burning topic which was worrying him very much.

Mrs Marconi came to school to explain the problem to me privately, woman to woman. Stephen was already twelve because his birthday fell early in the academic year and, given his above-average height, he was on the cusp of puberty. But one of his testicles was 'undescended'.

This is a condition which some boys are born with. The tiny testicle fails to drop into the scrotum in the last weeks of pregnancy as it should. Often it moves down of its own accord during infancy or childhood. But sometimes it doesn't and Stephen's was still retained above the scrotum in the wrong place – and the adolescent, genital growth spurt, which would turn this into a major medical problem with the potential to cause serious ruptures, was imminent.

So Stephen was about to have surgery to reposition his testicle where it should be. And the poor lad was nearly paralytic with embarrassment, first at the need to discuss it with me and second, probably worse, at the fear of the other boys finding out about it.

Once I was in the picture, we were able to handle his absence from school with the tact and diplomacy it needed. I think he knew that his mother had explained the truth to me but I never discussed it with Stephen directly. I was able, as well, to tell one or two trusted colleagues, such as Ian Castle, what was going on so that we could discreetly ensure that Stephen took things fairly easily for a week or two after his return to school. Stephen's testicle was my first real experience of practical pastoral work and advocacy. Odd that it should have been such a male issue, given my total lack of experience with boys.

Years later, one of my own sons was born with an undescended testicle. Remembering Stephen Marconi, I pushed and pushed the medical people to get it sorted while he was still young enough to take it in his stride. He eventually had the surgery when he was eight, much to my relief – and to the patient's when he grew up and realised how much more traumatic it would have been, had he been twelve like Stephen.

So these, and thirty-one others – there were thirty-five in the class – were the group who were to be the backbone of my first year in teaching. Someone, probably Ian Castle, had had the surprisingly sensible idea that I should teach them for several subjects. That meant that the boys saw me a lot and it made life for them seem a bit gentler and more like primary school. It also enabled me to establish myself very thoroughly with a group I could manage.

The upshot was that I taught 1B for fourteen periods a week. I took them for English, history, geography, RE (religious education) and form period – a weekly slot in which we could discuss and deal with form business.

The Creekside Comp week was divided into forty periods, of which I had just five 'free' – one a day if I was lucky, which usually I wasn't. The staff absentee rate was so high that we all had to cover unscheduled lessons all the time. And there were no concessions for me as a probationary newcomer.

Apart from 1B I was down to teach English to the parallel class, 1A, and a lower-stream class, 1D. I also acquired 2C for English and a couple of lessons a week each with two tricky, lower-stream second-year groups and, worst of all, with 3F for a double period on Friday afternoons. Hard to imagine what those men at the top were thinking about when they thought that this last was sensible timetabling for a newcomer. And, by today's standards, it was an unthinkably heavy timetable for a beginner.

3F, of whom more anon, was Geoff's own class and 'challenging' is hardly an adequate adjective to describe them.

CHAPTER FIVE

I got virtually no mentoring or advice apart from Geoff's cynical, funny, often protective but not always constructive, comments. My 'induction' to the English department was ten minutes in the stock cupboard with Ben Whittington, he who had kindly invited me to sit in on his lesson about flight the previous term.

Ben was a gifted teacher and a talented man in his late twenties. He had almost finished his external degree in economics at Goldsmiths when I first met him. He and Jack Rowlands had done this course together and become close friends. They also played golf at Beckenham Place Park every Saturday – sometimes with a third, youngish Creekside Comp colleague, Malcolm Drood, who was form teacher to 3E.

I liked Ben, who was to leave the school within a year or so for an academic job and major promotion. It was a given at Creekside Comp that staff who were any good disappeared rapidly for pastures with more potential. The rest were either so totally set in their ways that they lacked all ambition or they were useless.

Great sadness lay in Ben's future though. Shortly after he left the school, but before I did, he was driving his pregnant wife and their very young child along a motorway in the north of England when Mrs Whittington complained of a sudden and very severe headache. She died of a brain haemorrhage shortly after Ben had got her to the nearest hospital. He had just started a new job and had to leave his child, at least for a while, in the care of his sister whose home he then visited at weekends. All a dreadful tragedy.

At the beginning of my first full term though, Ben was simply a junior English teacher doing his bit to make sure this unlikely female recruit had some idea how to teach the classes she'd been given for better or for worse.

There was, of course, no syllabus. Creekside Comp's Head of English, Peter Beach, spent all his time doing important things in Upper School. He had no say in my appointment or role in the work I did. It was a long time before I knew who he was and even longer before I had a conversation with him.

'Now this is the book we usually use with B and C streams,' said Ben, handing me copies of *The Art of English 1G*, *2G* and *3G* published by Schofield and Sims. G stood for 'general'. There was also a parallel, more advanced series of books for 'top' streams, each of which had the prefix C for certificate but we didn't have those at Creekside Comp.

First published in 1965, the G course was written by Roger Mansfield, the C-level books by Keith Newson. One of them, or maybe both, taught, by coincidence, at Sedgehill School – one of ILEA's rather different, new purpose-built comprehensives and only three miles or so away in Bellingham, although I never met them.

Those books were to play a big and far-reaching part in my life. Since I was woefully undereducated to be teaching secondary school English, I used the books as the backbone of my teaching.

Keeping just a step or two ahead of the pupils, I consolidated all the basics of grammar which I needed to teach. Of course I'd done English grammar at both primary and secondary school – and I had the advantage of having done Latin – but my grasp of grammar was still patchy and often instinctive rather than systematic.

Mansfield ably filled in the gaping holes. And, as every teacher knows, there is no finer way of consolidating your own learning than by explaining or teaching the topic to someone else.

I knew little or nothing about suitable literature for young readers either. And this was a tremendous strength of Mansfield's books. Each book contained enough chapters to last throughout the school year if you did one every couple of weeks.

A suitable extract for the age group opened every chapter, followed by comprehension work with creative writing and grammar work loosely linked to whatever the extract was about. They were planned so that events such as bonfire night, Christmas and summer holidays fell at the right time so that users were reading topical material.

Book 1G opened with an extract from Erich Kastner's *Emil and the Detectives* – the account of Emil being robbed on the train on his way, unaccompanied, to 1930s Berlin. Later there was a lovely extract from *Rufus M* by Eleanor Estes about a child desperate to take out a library book, a piece from *The Railway Children* and another from *The Family from One End Street* – among many other delights. There were nice, understated woodcut drawings by Tom Wanless too.

With 1B I simply started at the beginning and worked through *The Art of English G1*. It was, in effect, my syllabus and it worked beautifully because both the boys and I knew exactly where we were.

Over thirty-five years and most of a teaching career later I was asked by a publisher to write some textbooks for 10-14-year-olds. What I produced – *So You Really Want to Learn English* Books 1, 2 and 3 and *Year 9 English* (Galore Park Publishing, now part of Hodder Education) – pays homage to the Mansfield/Newson format. I use a much wider range of extracts and build in much more emphasis on wider reading along with detailed work on grammar, spelling and punctuation, but the basic shape of my books is a passage and then other work linked to it. Thank you, Mr Mansfield.

Ben also gave me copies of *English Through Experience*, Creekside Comp's preferred textbook for top streams. I used it with classes such as 1A but never felt as comfortable with it as with *The Art of English* because the approach was woollier and less systematic.

There was no recommended book for lower streams, although Ben did point me towards one or two possibilities and advised me to experiment. Not very helpful for someone as woefully ill-equipped as I was. It made it much harder for me to be assertive and clear with those classes who were generally harder to handle anyway, so I tended to get off on the wrong foot with classes for whom I didn't have a decent textbook.

And what about literature? Wasn't I supposed to introduce the boys to Great Works as well? 'Yes, you'll want to keep a class reader going alongside the other work,' said Ben. There were copies of *Emil and the Detectives*, for example, which of course, at that stage I hadn't read. Ben thought it might work well with 1B since that was where *The Art of English* started and he turned out to be right, although it was never a book I was very taken with.

Much more exciting was spotting in the stock cupboard copies of *The Silver Sword* by Ian Seraillier. Now, in a moment of aberration my teacher training college had managed to do something useful in running a single half-day session in which three children's authors spoke to us. One of these was Ian Seraillier, who lived nearby in a Sussex village. The others were Rosemary Sutcliff (of *Eagle of the Ninth* fame) and Brian Wildsmith, a wonderfully vibrant illustrator who has written dozens of colourful books for very young children.

I hadn't, inevitably, read any of Seraillier's books, although I had, as a one-off *quid pro quo* project, helped teach one of his mini-operas for children in a Sussex primary school because I did music as a subsidiary subject at college.

College staff should have been sternly telling students intending to teach English to read at least two children's books a week and to be prepared to keep that knowledge up to date for decades to come – for as long as they remained in teaching, in fact. But they weren't. So here I was trying to find suitable books for these boys when the only writing I knew for young readers was the stuff I'd read in my own childhood.

But Seraillier's name caught my eye because I'd met him. I think *The Silver Sword* was the first children's book I ever read wearing my teacher's hat. I have read it dozens of times since and am still moved by it. The first time I read it with a class I discovered that I could not read the last chapter aloud without weeping. And I still can't. Since the first time was with 1B and we were rapidly learning to trust and respect each other I don't think their hearing the crack in my voice mattered much. In fact it probably helped to teach them that being moved by books is allowed. It's normal. It isn't something to marvel or sneer at.

Other books I used a lot in that first year or two as class readers included *Treasure Island*, which I never liked, although some of the boys seemed to. Arthur Conan-Doyle's short story 'Silver Blaze' – in which the odd thing Holmes notices is the famous dog which does not bark – went down reasonably well. So did Alan Garner's *Elidor*, which was then hot-off-the-press. We also had another Ian Seraillier novel, *Flight to Adventure*, which was a readable second world war spy/adventure story, but nothing like as good as *The Silver Sword* with all that wonderful human interest. I suppose that's why it seems long since to have disappeared, whereas *The Silver Sword* is alive and well and has never been out of print. It has also been variously dramatised over the years.

Something else no one at college ever mentioned was the vexed question of covering for absent colleagues and we did an enormous amount of it at Creekside Comp, where absenteeism was always rampant.

Although I had five periods a week when I wasn't timetabled to teach, I could never rely on getting that time for marking or anything else. From the very beginning I routinely 'lost' my 'free' time.

Jack Rowlands or, on the rare occasions he appeared, Jim O'Riordan, would fill in the dreaded cover slip as soon as he knew who wasn't coming in to work that day. It was simply a blank timetable with one's name at the top and the lesson, or even lessons in the plural, which one was required to cover that day filled in on the chart. They were usually sent round by 'boy messenger' and the sight of a lad at the door clutching an ominous piece of paper always sent my heart plummeting southwards.

I found it difficult enough to teach – or at least contain – the boys in my own lessons. Trying to do it as a one-off with classes where I knew no names was usually a demoralising experience and an educational travesty.

For a start it was never one's own subject. The lessons to be covered were always maths, history or some mysterious subject I'd never heard of such as technical drawing or mechanics. Needless to say, these were never planned absences and there was never – not once in all the years I was at Creekside Comp – any work sent in by the absentee teacher for the class to do in his absence. Neither did any head of department or head-of-subject-in-Lower-School show the slightest interest in some Tom, Dick or Harriet ordered to teach his subject. You were utterly and completely on your own.

For about a week, or maybe two, I harboured the puritanical notion that if a period was billed as, say, RE, then it behoved me to try to do something vaguely related to that subject. I soon abandoned it in favour of a couple of things I discovered which might actually tame the hordes for a few minutes.

The first was the power of the short story. I quickly taught myself to read aloud reasonably well. Although I'd been hopeless at it at school, it's a real survival skill for an English teacher and I'd soon perfected it. I think I found it easier when I could practise in the privacy of a classroom without peers to make me self-conscious.

I found Bill Naughton's book of short stories, *The Goalkeeper's Revenge*, in the school library and first picked it up because I assumed it was about football and therefore might appeal to the male youth of Deptford.

Actually those thirteen warm, lively stories set in the 1930s in the Lancashire of Naughton's boyhood are not about football at all – not even the lead story which has the f-word in its title. And those compelling tales live on. *The Goalkeeper's Revenge* was republished in the Bloomsbury Reader series in October 2011.

I carried the book around in my bag and whenever I was asked to cover a lesson I would tell them that we weren't going to do maths or whatever. Instead I was going to read them a story. In return for being 'let off' the subject I wanted them to sit quietly and listen. It wasn't foolproof but more often than not it worked. I loved (and still love) Naughton's 'Spit Nolan', 'Seventeen Oranges' and 'The Well-off Kid'. And so, apparently, did most of the listeners. At least some of the time.

I also made, quite by chance, the unlikely discovery that 1960s teenage boys adored Kipling's 'Rikki Tiki Tavi' from *The Jungle Book* and 'The Elephant's Child' from the *Just So Stories*. I went on reading both those to classes of all types and levels – and both sexes – for the next thirty years and they were invariably received in rapt silence. Old-fashioned, politically incorrect stories as they both are, there's something about Kipling's narrative thrust and prose rhythms which grabs children.

No one ever queried or mentioned what I was doing in Creekside Comp cover lessons. Like everyone else on the premises I was simply managing my own survival. Had I been challenged, I suppose I might have said that it was an educational bonus for these boys to be exposed to good stories which would indirectly benefit their language skills. Or maybe I couldn't have articulated that in my first term.

The only flaw in the strategy was that I often covered the same class at the same time week after week – especially if it 'belonged' to Pat McGuire, for example. It meant that I had to remember to take a different story, although occasionally a group would ask me to do a repeat because they'd enjoyed it so much first time. Gratifying – even when gnashing one's teeth with fury about having to cover for malingerers.

From the very first week I had to teach a full timetable. There was no remission for being what was then called a 'probationary' teacher. Today teachers in their first year working towards what is now clumsily known as 'qualified teacher status' usually have light timetables, with time set aside to work with a mentor – a formally designated senior colleague. There was nothing remotely like that at Creekside Comp. As Geoff once said, 'As long as you don't actually kill a boy no one will ever darken your door and interfere with what you're doing. Once you've shut the classroom door you're on your own in this place.'

Everyone had to do playground duty every week too – as if all those lessons weren't enough. I was paired with a very pleasant, wise, fatherly, calm maths teacher called Andy. Actually his name was John Andrews but everyone, even his wife, called him Andy. He had, like my father and so many men in their generation, served in the war and then done the one-year 'emergency' teacher training in the late 1940s. The scheme produced some of the best teachers who ever graced the profession.

Andy and I had to take our cups of tea into the huge bleak playground during the morning and afternoon breaks where we'd chat and keep an eye on the hundreds of boys running amok – usually with footballs – as far away from staff cars as we could shepherd them.

We – or rather Andy – often had to break up fights. Someone would shout 'Bundle!' and the whole of Lower School would, as one, encircle two boys wanting, apparently, to tear each other limb from limb like gladiators in a Roman amphitheatre and with an audience nearly as big. Andy was very skilled at defusing such explosive situations. I think it was partly because he was so calm and softly spoken. He also had a natural authority, developed, perhaps, during his war years.

At the end of break Andy blew a whistle and we oversaw the boys lining up in forms before we sent them line by line into the building. I suppose that's why the scent-of-Deptford lavatories were where they were. It meant boys could use them from the playground.

We had to do the same thing for half of the lunch break – about thirty-five minutes. There were two sittings for lunch – universally known as 'dinner' – and boys went to one or the other. When we were on playground duty Andy and I went to the second sitting in the huge canteen which Andy called 'the piggery', sadly with good reason. These boys definitely did not have middle class table manners. There was a lot of shouting, unprepossessing gobbling and spilling of food. Pretty it wasn't and Andy, an old-fashioned gentleman in many ways, was always apologetic about my having to go into the canteen at all.

There was, at this point, a quiet, separate dining room for staff but when we were on playground duty it was part of our job to be in the canteen for the second half of the dinner hour, supervising as we ate. Andy hated it. In practice it usually meant that neither he nor I ate anything much on our duty days, although the food wasn't bad, and when I could eat them in private, I quite enjoyed Creekside Comp school dinners.

In what little spare time I had – the occasional 'free' period (if Pat McGuire actually came to work, for example), during the lunch break and after school – I explored fascinating Deptford, which was at the end of an era, although I don't think I realised that at the time.

In the late 1960s it was still a tight community based on the High Street. Streets of small Victorian terraced houses ran off the High Street. They would originally have been the homes of food factory workers. Deptford was once the centre for the slaughter of imported livestock, brought in by river. In the nineteenth century thousands, including women and children, worked in the gutting shops. Deptford also had several big industrial flour mills, the last of which, Robinsons, was still operational when I arrived there.

There was a strong sense of nearly everyone knowing nearly everyone else despite the thousands of immigrants from the Caribbean, India, Africa, Turkey and many other places who were living there too by the late '60s.

But, things were changing fast. Many houses were, when I knew them, generally pretty run down and poor, and 'slum clearance' initiatives were afoot to get rid of them and build 'nice modern flats' instead. That would, very soon, mean 'incomers', a different demographic dynamic and, eventually, the almost complete disappearance of the Deptford I knew.

Many of the people – including the boys at Creekside Comp – who lived in those streets, belonged to families who had lived in Deptford for generations. They manned market stalls on the High Street or traded in scrap metal. Some of the older, indigenous Deptfordians – despite the station with a ten-minute service to Waterloo in the centre of the High Street – had never been out of Deptford. And that wasn't just a legend. Whenever we took a party of boys into central London there would always be gasps of awe from some lads as we crossed Westminster Bridge or skirted Trafalgar Square because they had never seen it before.

I did a lot of shopping in Deptford High Street. I liked the salt-of-the-earth straightforwardness of shopkeepers such as the greengrocer who had a notice up saying 'Rhubarb for regularity'. I got to know the cheerful Deptford woman who ran the newsagents. The clothes shops were entertaining too.

One evening Nick picked me up after school and we bought my wedding ring – which I still wear, of course – in a Deptford High Street jewellers, not a national chain, where I had spotted one I really liked.

The two hormone-laden boys, third years I think, who ogled and made faces through the shop door and tapped at it throughout the purchase couldn't believe their luck. I didn't actually know them but they must have known me by sight from school. It might have been better if we'd slipped into Deptford on a Saturday for that particular bit of shopping rather than pick the moment when hundreds of Creekside Comp boys had just been set loose. But I still hadn't learnt to anticipate what excites teenage boys.

Between the school and the High Street was the exquisite Georgian terrace, Albury Street, which I frequently walked along en route for the shops. In the flurry of 1960s architectural vandalism many people wanted it razed to make room for new buildings. Fortunately the conservation lobby, at a time when their stance was much less fashionable than it is now, fought hard. They won and Albury Street is still there today.

The alternative route to the High Street was via St Paul's churchyard. St Paul's Deptford is a magnificent Thomas Archer church – a reminder of how prosperous Deptford once was – which people still visit from far and wide. Its rector, when I worked at Creekside Comp, was George Gould, who wore a toupée which made us giggle. He came into school regularly – often for lunch. 'Wherever there's free food there's always a clergyman,' said Geoff, insouciantly writing off any genuine pastoral efforts George might, just possibly, have been making.

In many ways Deptford was deeply old-fashioned. Outside St Paul's I once saw a very young, quite scruffy and poor-looking couple waiting with their baby. She was about to go into the building to be 'churched' – ritualistically cleansed of the sin of childbirth according to the (Anglican) Book of Common Prayer so that she could, once again, receive communion. Her husband – they would undoubtedly have been married – was obviously there to look after the child while his wife went into the church for her appointment with the man Geoff often referred to as 'the witch doctor'.

Inch by inch, crisis by crisis, term wore on. At half term Nick and I slipped off to the Isle of Wight for a few days, masquerading as Mr and Mrs Elkin as hotels expected you to do in those days – although I didn't bother with the traditional curtain ring on my wedding finger.

In November I took and passed my driving test which meant that occasionally – very grown up – I could borrow Nick's Morris 1000 and drive myself into school.

CHAPTER SIX

I began my second term in style – by missing most of the first fortnight. After a day or two back at the chalk face I succumbed to one of the nastiest doses of flu I have ever had. New teachers in a school are always vulnerable because they haven't had time to build up immunity to the bugs the children bring in. So it was a textbook case.

I spent a week in bed, ably nursed by my mother, as if I were six years old again. She even summoned the doctor, as you could then and my mother had always done if one of us was ill. For several days I was almost unable to stand, with high temperature, severe headaches, raging thirst and loss of appetite and, even after I managed to get vertical, I was pretty wobbly for a while.

Of course it wasn't my fault but I felt very guilty about it. First, I really didn't like not being at school and kept thinking about Pat McGuire and what my colleagues would be saying when they had to cover my lessons. Actually I don't suppose they were saying anything of the sort since my very polite and reasonable mother had phoned in on my behalf to explain, and sent my profuse apologies. And by then I think those men knew that I was no malingerer. But it didn't stop me fretting at the time.

The other reason that I felt so wretched about taking this nasty Deptford flu bug home was that, as soon as I'd recovered, my parents both went down with it. It was almost unheard of for my father to take time off work and it was the only time in their entire fifty-one-year marriage and business partnership that they both took to bed in a darkened room at the same time – not seeming to care for a day or two who was running their shop or indeed whether it was even open. It was quite out of character. They must have felt even worse than I had the previous week. A pretty virulent bug.

Back at school there was a flurry of excitement over the sudden disappearance of a PE instructor called Trevor Leigh. He was unmarried, unpopular and unqualified. His unqualified status meant that, officially, he had to be an instructor rather than a teacher, but in practice he was just another teacher on the staff.

The boys were very scathing about him, not least because he was very free with the 'slipper' – a hard-soled plimsoll with which it was still legal to whack offending children on the bottom. And his approach to PE was that – long gone, thank goodness – old-fashioned, quasi-military, sadistic, unfeeling way of doing things. He had no truck with 'softness'. Hard-bitten as most of them were, the staff didn't like Trevor much either.

He had, for some time, been friendly with the family of one of the boys in the third year, something which his colleagues found a bit odd and unhealthy. The family was about to emigrate to Australia.

One Monday morning we came into school to discover that Trevor, without telling anyone what he was going to do or giving notice at work, had simply upped stumps and gone to Australia with the boy and his family. They had sailed during the weekend so it was a *fait accompli*.

Cue for bemused and, in some cases, ribald, comments from Creekside Comp staff and some very puzzled questions from boys. That morning, a twinkle in his eye, Jack Rowlands announced that the hymn in assembly would be 'Eternal Father, strong to save/ whose arm doth bind the restless wave'.

Of course the boys, who didn't at that stage even know that Trevor had gone, weren't in on the joke but I could neither catch

Jack's eye nor sing, with a straight face, the refrain 'for those in peril on the sea'.

One of the odd things about daily life at Creekside Comp was that, although I was the most junior person on the staff, we were a united bunch in Lower School and nothing much seemed to be kept from me.

Things were openly discussed in the staffroom by Jack Rowlands and others, which would, in most other schools have been mentioned only in hushed tones behind closed doors. The omniscient Geoff didn't do secrets either.

So I knew all about Trevor Leigh's peculiar and sudden disappearance as soon as it had happened. Was he gay? Probably. Was he what my 1960s, call-a-spade-a-spade, blunt colleagues called a 'pervert' with designs on little boys and their juvenile whackable bottoms? More than likely. The alarming thing is that nobody seemed very bothered about it. His paedophilia, if that's what it was, was effectively – and shockingly from a modern perspective – condoned by the school and even by the family he emigrated with. The school and its pupils were certainly well shot of him, but of course the situation should not have been allowed to drift on until he scarpered of his own accord. It was an extreme example of Creekside Comp's dangerously casual attitude to boys' welfare.

I also knew about the charismatic, intriguing Robert Wells who appeared one day via Divisional Office to teach history and geography. He was a dark-haired, conventionally good-looking twenty-something man with an attractive speaking voice, a compelling manner and a good degree. He seemed to go down well with the boys and could manage even quite difficult classes, apparently effortlessly.

He had a good line in stories too. He told us in the staffroom one day that his sister worked as a prostitute and that, presumably, only in her twenties, she had managed to amass enough tax-free money to buy a house for cash. He was convincing enough and I more or less believed this tale. In view of what happened later it was probably true.

Robert Wells stayed for a term or two and then moved on, or was moved on by Divisional Office. He was only a temporary fill-in after all.

Then one day there was an alarmed and alarming call from County Hall – the central hub of ILEA, now an aquarium, home of the London Dungeon and a hotel on the south bank of the Thames. If Creekside Comp were to receive any approaches from Robert Wells seeking work then UNDER NO CIRCUMSTANCES was he to be employed or even allowed on the premises. For the laid-back late 1960s it was an extraordinarily unequivocal pronouncement.

In almost any other school I would not have known about that phone call but at chummy Creekside Comp Lower School it was common knowledge and the talk of the staffroom. One colleague who had a law degree summed it up laconically: 'There's only one question,' he said. 'Boys or girls?'

Several years later there was a high-profile scandal about a paedophile ring with detailed accounts of the trial in all the newspapers. One of the accused had the same name as Robert Wells and, although I never saw a corroborative photograph, I am pretty sure it was the same man whose sister had earned her house on her back. Pity. He was actually a rather good teacher. I hope he did some useful education work to help others in prison.

It was in that second term that I learned an important lesson about culture and dialect. Every single boy at Creekside Comp routinely used the singular verb form with the plural pronoun when using the verb 'to be'. In other words they said 'we was'. And they said it dozens of times every day. Since we tend to write what we say and hear they often wrote it too.

For months I corrected it whenever I heard a boy say 'we was', as well, obviously, as drawing attention to it in written work.

One day a slightly older boy – a second or third year, I think – had had enough. 'Look, Miss,' he said politely but assertively, 'I don't know where you come from but in Deptford we say "we was".'

Pause for thought. Although it went totally against everything I'd ever been taught about 'correct' English, I could see that, actually, this young man was right. And many years later when I read David Crystal's books about language and studied the concept of dialect, accent and non-standard forms I thought about that lad. 'Correctness', I came to realise, is not an absolute concept, although, of course, most of us know what we mean by 'standard English'.

At the time I felt humbled by the boy's reasonableness and proposed the obvious compromise: that he write 'we were' in essays and other written work but continue to use 'we was' in everyday transactional speech if he wished. And I stopped correcting it when I heard it.

Not that spoken English is free from pitfalls and misunderstandings. In my grammar school I was once reprimanded for addressing the Headmistress too casually. I had gone to her office to ask her for or about something. When I left I thanked her and said, 'Bye, Miss Harper.' She rounded on me asking, 'Do you realise what you just said?' and pointed out to me why such 'sloppy speech' was unacceptable from a pupil addressing a member of staff.

Well, she had a point, perhaps, but it's a good job she wasn't around to hear the boys of 1B sauntering into our classroom in the mornings or before lessons and saying, 'Wotcha, Miss.' At first it grated but I soon realised that they weren't being rude or disrespectful. It was simply the Deptford way of doing things. And it was friendly and a sign they were accepting me. It was their dialect and who was I to criticise it? Another lesson for me about the slippery nature of language and its use in different contexts.

Meanwhile I was still struggling with the novelty of adult status. When there was an accident in the playground in which a large, portly boy of fourteen broke some front teeth, I had a free period and no one else was around. By chance, I also had our car there, having driven in for once rather than coming in with Geoff.

Jack Rowlands, who was as usual in charge of Lower School at the time, asked me to drive the injured boy to the emergency dental clinic in Deptford and wait there with him *in loco parentis* until his mum turned up.

Of course, I looked after the weeping distressed lad as best I could, although he and I were complete strangers to each other. His mouth must have been extremely painful and he was very frightened. Maybe Jack also thought a bit of female caring was called for, which is why he assigned the job to me. It certainly must have looked that way to the dentist. I was twenty-two and the patient a strapping fourteen. 'Are you this boy's mother?' he demanded. I hope it was because he hadn't looked at me properly rather than that he thought I'd been the youngest child/mum in history.

1B and I continued to get to know each other. Take Brian Penny, for example. He was very small for his age and had a nice open freckly face. He was the only child of a widowed mother with whom he lived in a modest, privately rented flat in Lewisham. Like Mark Shaw, with whom he became close friends partly because they lived along the same bus route, Brian had been directed to Creekside Comp rather than his mother having chosen it.

He wasn't particularly good at academic work but Brian had heaps of common sense and was very reliable. He worked hard and conscientiously too. Able to chat to me comfortably as he probably had with his primary school teacher, he was the sort of boy who, because he didn't quite fit the Deptford mould, could easily have been bullied. But somehow he found the confidence to sail over the possibility – in his unassuming open way – so that it never happened.

Brian Penny and Mark Shaw were a good team – with a group of other boys they were pally with – throughout their years at

Creekside Comp and I often wonder whether they remained friends after they left school.

Another boy who was a character and very much his own man was Francis Grayson. He was tubby, forthright and ginger-haired. You could always rely on Francis for surprisingly mature, articulate contributions to classroom discussion. 'Well, I think you just have to accept that human beings have supremacy over animals,' he said once, aged about twelve, in an interchange about animal rights arising out of something we'd all read together in class. 'If you don't it's going to affect so many other things that life would be impossible.'

Then there was Paul Collier who was deeply in love with London buses. He was a bright boy who used beautiful and immaculate italic handwriting. It was fashionable then to teach the italic style in primary school. Most children didn't fully master it and ended up with disastrous scrappy handwriting. Paul was the exception. He could write in the italic style with speed and panache. I expect he still does.

But it was the buses which really turned him on. He knew every bus route and every depot and terminus. He spent his weekends, like John Betjeman with the Underground, travelling new (to him) bus routes to find out more. If there'd been an A Level in London Bus Studies, Paul would have passed it with the top grade at age eleven. If you wanted information about a bus it was quicker to ask Paul than to look it up – which would have been very laborious in those pre-internet days. When he left school he went to work for London Transport. How could they fail to take him? I'm sure he was a great asset to his employer.

Meanwhile at home my mother and I – that's how it was done in those days – were organising The Wedding at the end of March. And there was a problem about the date. Twelve months earlier we had booked 29 March, long before I knew I was going to work at Creekside Comp, on the assumption that wherever I was working, the Saturday before the Easter weekend would fall in the holidays.

We were wrong. ILEA schools didn't break up until the Tuesday of Easter week when I would be away on honeymoon. Like the church, caterers and printing, our week in Paris had been booked months before. So I sought advice from Mr Baker and Jack Rowlands.

They told me that I'd have to apply formally to ILEA for two days' unpaid leave of absence. I think they probably put in a good word for me because I was granted the time off very readily.

Geoff, in his gruff way, seemed to take a dimish view of all this. A great believer in marriage he had, or said he had, no time for weddings. He told me more than once that he and Coral had travelled to the register office by bus, signed the papers with two unknown witnesses and then moved in together. Why anyone needed a tiresome clergyman, a party and an expensive holiday was, he protested, incomprehensible.

That's why I didn't invite him and Coral to the wedding. I honestly thought that he wouldn't want to come. In fact looking back now, of course, I realise he'd have been delighted, although those proverbial wild horses would never have dragged that out of him.

Instead, just before I got out of his car the last time I saw him before the Big Day, he presented me with a large casserole dish all wrapped up appropriately. Almost overwhelmed – and very surprised – I stammered my thanks to which he said tersely, 'Nonsense! You're one of the nicest girls I've met for years.'

I really wish, with hindsight, that I'd had the wisdom to recognise that he didn't always quite mean some of the more outrageous things he said, and invited Geoff and Coral to St George's Church on 29 March 1969 with a reception in the church hall afterwards.

What happened at school before my wedding was, to me, almost unbelievable and very heart-warming. As term wore on I knew 1B were up to something because one of them audibly dropped a tin of money on the floor during the register one morning. It was followed by looks of horrified silence. My instinct told me to say nothing and continue with the register.

They gave me a china table lamp with mock rococo decoration and a pink plastic lampshade. They'd collected the money themselves and made the purchase, helped by someone's mum, I suspect, at British Home Stores in Lewisham. The gift spoke more for their taste than mine, but I was very moved by what it said about their relationship with me after only two terms. There was a card they'd all signed too. It was the first time I ever shed a proper tear in a classroom – which pleased the boys who immediately knew they'd done the right thing. I bet they all went home and told their mothers that evening how pleased and overcome Miss Hillyer had been. 'She cried, Mum!'

The staff, meanwhile, had also collected for a gift, rather more discreetly. Given that I'd only been there two terms that was quite something too. I never found out who instigated and organised it but it was Jim O'Riordan, in school for a day or two to everyone's surprise, who took me aside to ask what I'd like. I chose a Bex Bissell floor sweeper and – because there was some money left over – everyday repeat-line wine glasses, one or two of which I still have, from Habitat.

Jim also thought – he liked and believed in weddings as strongly as Geoff purported not to – I shouldn't work until 4pm the day before my wedding and offered me the Friday off unofficially on top of the two days the following week I'd already negotiated.

Given Jim's own attitude, distorted by illness, to attendance at work and the school's staff absentee problems this was pretty absurd. I know several colleagues disapproved of Jim's 'dropping in' and casually offering unnecessary time off to staff. Nonetheless I accepted gratefully, partly because I hadn't the maturity to see the issues. Looking back, it really wouldn't have hurt me or made any difference to the wedding arrangements if I'd worked that Friday.

So it was on Thursday 27th that I was feted with all my gifts and good wishes.

Saturday 29th went very happily and according to plan, with me in my £16 wedding dress, having washed my own hair and done my own makeup in the morning. How times change. We entertained seventy or so guests for a 'buffet lunch' (aka sandwiches in 1969) before changing clothes, in the old-fashioned no-discos-then style, and being driven to Heathrow by a friend.

My new passport was dated from that day and was in my married name – another old-fashioned custom which seems to have gone. I also wore a suit and a hat. The passport checker at the airport congratulated us.

When we returned from Paris, on Easter Monday, Nick and I had ten days to settle into our flat before my new term started.

It was a spacious, unfurnished, two-bedroom flat in a block of Victorian mansion flats in the middle of a large estate of such buildings in Forest Hill. Our flat was on the ground floor and we had French doors leading from one of the rooms into a small private garden.

Although this was 1969, it might as well have been 1920. The estate was managed by an eccentric old chap who'd married the granddaughter of the late-Victorian entrepreneur who built it. My maternal grandmother knew him and had put in a word for us.

We'd had tenancy for a few weeks and done a bit of decorating in advance but our landlord was a Victorian at heart and determined that there was going to be no moving in until after the Big Day.

It was a good flat – our first child would eventually be born in it – but the estate was somewhat run down by the time we lived in it and was sold on to developers before we left the flat five years later. We had to get used to the vagaries of the hot water system, which was meant to be included in the rent but sometimes failed for as long as three weeks at a time. We got very used to visiting friends and family with a wash bag in hand. 'Could I have a quick bath while I'm here?'

Then there was the estate's ancient odd-job man, whom we called 'John the Bodger'. He appeared to have worked there since the estate was built.

Nonetheless it was our home and we regarded ourselves as very lucky to have it – at an absurdly low rent which had to be paid quarterly in the traditional, but by then almost unheard of, way. We paid £75 on Lady Day (25 March), Midsummer (24 June), Michaelmas (25 September) and Christmas Day.

I was earning about £60 net per month and Nick a little more when we first married. So that £300 per year for rent was about a fifth of our income and therefore manageable.

The flat was just over a mile from both my parents and Nick's and we had many other relations and friends within walking distance. We were also living next door to the church that I had attended with my grandparents right through childhood and at whose youth club Nick and I had originally met. So, although neither of us attended church anymore we already knew many of our new neighbours. Suburban London it might have been but it was very much like a village, surrounded as we were by contacts and connections who'd known our families, in some cases, through three or more generations.

Within two days of getting back from Paris and moving in I was ill again – with a nasty tummy bug which I had presumably picked up in France. This time it was my mother-in-law who took charge and called (her) doctor to whom we subsequently transferred.

There was concern because I was a teacher. One of the local infant schools – by coincidence it was the one I'd attended myself – had had a serious dysentery outbreak at the end of the spring term. In order to prevent it spreading, ILEA had closed the school for over a week before Easter.

My closest friend – we'd been to secondary school together – taught infants in the dysentery-affected school having started there when I went to Creekside Comp. There were fears that maybe that connection had spread the disease to me, although my friend had managed, by practising very careful hygiene, to avoid getting it herself and I hadn't seen her since the Wedding Day anyway. So the worry was a red herring but it shows how seriously the medical people were taking it.

After a couple of days I was back to normal and busy sorting out my new home, unpacking and finding places for wedding presents, writing thank you letters and – what delicious novelty – cooking supper ready for when Nick got home from his Lewisham Borough Council job.

Then it was back to school for the summer term. As Mrs Elkin.

CHAPTER SEVEN

The boys adapted to it effortlessly. It was as if they'd never addressed me as anything else.

They were funny, though, about their vision of my married life. I made no secret of the fact that Nick and I have very little interest in television. For our first seven or eight years together we didn't even own a set and to this day we rarely bother with more than an hour or two a week.

So 1B knew that there was no TV in the new Elkin home because it was one of the things I'd chatted about. I read lots of books instead and would try gently to encourage the boys to detach themselves occasionally from TV and try the joys of the printed word.

One day Terry Worthington asked me very seriously about something which had evidently been worrying him: 'Miss, what does your husband do on Saturday afternoons?'

I was puzzled. 'What do you mean, what does he do?' I said. 'He might do all sorts of things – like read the paper, visit his parents, go shopping, do some jobs in the house. It just depends.'

Terry persisted: 'No, I mean what does he DO? About the football?' Then the penny dropped. In his entire life Terry had never met, or heard of, an adult male who didn't spend Saturday afternoons watching football on television. So it was inconceivable that his teacher's husband could be any different.

I was educating them in more ways than I knew.

1B continued to be the great delight in my life but Mrs Elkin didn't find it any easier to manage second and third years than Miss Hillyer had.

And it was partly because of my legs, had I but realised it at the time. I have always had a habit of perching either on the edge of my own teacher's desk or, if it isn't occupied, on one of the pupils' desks. It's a nice informal stance, without physical barriers, for reading aloud or leading a discussion. But you are still sitting at a physically higher level than the pupils so you can see all your charges. I did it for decades in the girls' schools I taught in later and thought nothing of it.

It was different at Creekside Comp where it seems that for some boys the very sight of me sent adolescent hormones racing. Half a lifetime later I enjoyed a cup of tea and a long chat in Costa with a former Creekside boy who was in 1A. 'In 1968,' he said, 'every boy in the school fancied either you or the French teacher Mrs Scott and there was a lot of rivalry between the two groups. When one of you walked down the main stairs at break, boys would jostle to see who could get the best view. It ruled our lives.'

He also told me that there was competitiveness in the classroom to see who could get the best and most central seat in order to look up my 1960s short skirt when I sat on the desk at the front. Perhaps it's an indication of how much it mattered to them that they ensured I never got wind of what was going on. Had I realised that I was providing a peep show I'd never have sat on a desk again. I blush now to think how innocent I must have been and what must have been said amongst the boys in private.

No wonder I had difficulty maintaining discipline. Another part of the problem was the lack of structure and resources for the lower-ability classes. They were effectively written off by many staff – seen as boys who were time-serving until their sixteenth birthday. And often they disappeared on the day to no one's regret. There was very little teacherly respect for anything as tidy as the beginnings and endings across most of the Deptford community.

I managed to tame one lower-ability second-year group – a little but it wasn't great – by making comprehension work cards for them. I spent hours writing out short factual pieces with illustrations cut, for example, from magazines. Then I added questions and tasks.

There were about twenty in the class. At least class numbers were smaller in the lower streams. Someone in a decision-making seat had had that much sense at least. I reckoned that if I made twenty cards it would give me twenty lessons because we could rotate them.

It actually worked quite well and I must, rather more by luck than judgement, have got the level about right because most of the boys settled down to their cards quite happily. Perhaps they appreciated the effort I'd put in. After all I had no IT to help and each one took an hour or so to create. They certainly didn't deface them which was, in itself, something of an achievement.

My worst weekly hurdle was 3F. They were huge beefy lads who would look down on me with terrifying, knowing, sneers. They knew only two sorts of women: mothers (and other maternal or sisterly relations) and tarts. And they couldn't pigeonhole me in either slot so they circled round me like hyenas sensing my ignorance and lack of confidence, but also half aware of the adult men in the building who would forcibly protect me if the boys pushed their luck too far.

Whoever devised the timetable which gave 3F to me, a dangerously inexperienced young woman still in her first year, for a double lesson on a Friday afternoon, surely needed urgent treatment. Or at least to be sent on a timetabling course.

It was, anyway, one of those unhappy timetable muddles. I wasn't 3F's regular English teacher. They were – because their needs were a pretty low priority – split between two English teachers and there was little or no liaison between us. I simply had to try and contain them somehow for an hour and ten minutes. *Sauve qui peut.*

I often found myself trying to keep them in the room when it wasn't Friday afternoon too. They frequently turned up on the dreaded 'cover sheet' because whoever was meant to be teaching them was missing. And it really made no difference which subject they were meant to be getting, it was a cross between babysitting and guard duty, very badly done in my case.

Not all staff regarded them as a lost cause. Geoff was 3F's form teacher and he was good with this group of about fifteen boys. They were the bottom stream, as there was no 3G that year.

However irreverently he joked about them in the staffroom or in the car on the way to and from school, he actually liked most of them in his gruff, unspoken way, although even he found it very hard work. In their turn, unsurprisingly, the majority of 3F thought Mr Miles was 'all right' – the greatest of Deptford accolades. They trusted him and they knew that, at heart, he was on their side and that whatever else, he would always be fair.

Take the reasonably cheerful 3F boy who was the son of a Turkish food street trader and relatively affable with me, if a bit over-familiar. One day, annoyed with one of his classmates, he brought a huge fearsome-looking knife to school. He'd nicked it from his dad. It didn't take Geoff long to rumble what was brewing. He disarmed the boy without fuss or reporting it to anyone and, for some reason, gave me the knife to look after which is why I remember it.

Sammy Wright, a thin weasly boy with a sinister glint in his eye, was the most notorious 3F member. He was talked about a lot in the staffroom and, frankly, he scared me stiff. I could sometimes just about hold the group for a few minutes occasionally if Wright was absent, as he often was. With Wright present I stood no chance at all. He only had to look at me with an insolent toss of the head and every boy in the class would be behind him. Flanked by his henchmen, one of whom was a huge, tough, shark-like black boy whose unlikely Shakespearean surname was Casca, Wright controlled the class as effectively as any adult East End gang leader would.

When the Education Welfare Officer – EWO but still referred to by Geoff and others as the 'School Board Man' – visited, Janet and Margaret would ply him with tea in the office. If he was in a kind mood he would sometimes agree not to find time to visit the Wright household and drive the truanting Sammy back into school for a day or two. He knew how seriously we needed the break.

Although Sammy was the only Wright I knew, he came from a long line of troublesome (and troubled?) brothers well known to the police and every other agency in the district. Geoff and older colleagues had been struggling with Wrights for years. And the further down the family you went the more serious the problems. One of Sammy's younger brothers was found guilty of murder after I'd left the school.

The father of this alarming tribe, 'Old Man Wright', as he was known in the staffroom, could be found every day after work drinking in the notorious Robin Hood and Little John in Deptford Church Street, the site of many an ugly brawl. The council demolished the pub when Church Street was widened and improved in the 1980s. I half suspect that its condemnation was just an unsubtle way of dealing with the Wrights – although to quote one of Geoff's memorable aphorisms, that would only have been like trying to cure measles by scratching off the spots.

More than twenty years later when I was teaching in a girls' school in Chatham we brought in a mobile bookshop housed in a decommissioned bus. It came from London and it was part of our book festival. The bus driver had retired from his London Transport job and now just drove this rather novel book bus to venues part-time.

He was a Deptford man. When I took him a cup of tea and some lunch – because he couldn't leave the bus and its valuable stock unmanned – we got chatting about the families I remembered. Oh yes – the Wrights! So many boys. So much trouble. So much influence. To all intents and purposes a Deptfordian mini-mafia.

It was good to hear it from someone who'd lived among them, and now and then even shared a jar with Old Man Wright in the Robin Hood and Little John.

Just occasionally someone stood up to Sammy Wright. Robert Higgins was a very large – tall and broad as well as overweight – boy with glasses. I found him a tricky comedian to handle in class but he wasn't aggressive. He was tidily dressed but pretty laid back and happy to go with the murky 3F flow – usually.

Then came the day when someone in 3F casually, but deliberately, hurled a broken bottle over the high back wall of the playground during break. There were council houses behind the school and their small gardens abutted the school wall. Sitting in her garden, on this occasion, unseen by any of the boys, was a woman feeding a baby. The missile missed them by inches.

Once she'd recovered from what could have been a very nasty incident the woman, very reasonably, phoned the school to complain. Everyone knew it was 3F because they'd been playing and fooling about as a group in the bit of the yard which they, and everyone else, regarded as 'their' territory. The question was which boy had thrown the bottle?

Most of the staff could have guessed accurately. So could the rest of the school. And every one of the 3F boys knew for a fact it was Wright. But Deptfordians don't 'grass' and they were very much under Wright's control anyway. So when questioned as a group, they simply blanked as one solid entity and no one said a word... except one.

Higgins went straight to Geoff. 'It was Wright, sir.' He came straight out with it, according to what Geoff told me later. 'I wouldn't normally grass and I'm loyal to me mates but not when there's a little baby involved.'

He was all of thirteen and growing up in an environment which would have made the original blackboard jungle look like a Glyndebourne supper party. Higgins was also deemed 'dim' by the powers that be. They'd put him in 3F, after all. But here he was making mature, independent and courageous moral judgements.

'Higgins is a decent kid,' said Geoff, educating me on the way home in his usual way. 'One day he'll have a wife and children and bring them all up to be as decent as he is. He can't help being stuck in a place like this with a gang like 3F but he'll rise above it.'

Geoff also thought that the rest of his motley group had been quietly quite relieved that Higgins – who asked for no secrecy – had taken action so firmly. None of them would have had the courage, but somewhere in their hearts most of them knew he'd done the right thing. And much as they fawned round him, few 3F boys actually liked Wright. It also meant that the identity of the culprit was no longer in doubt and the other boys were exonerated.

As the end of the summer term approached, someone senior on the staff died. Because he was a head of department based in the other building I couldn't even visualise him, which says a lot about the way the school was still being disparately mismanaged across two sites with little or no sense of unity.

We'd had just two whole-school staff meetings since I'd started there almost a year before. Of course that wasn't anything like enough even to mean that I recognised all colleagues by sight. And I certainly didn't know all their names.

On one occasion the Head of RE appeared in our staffroom when there was no one there except me. So I offered him a cup of tea and asked him if he'd come far or some such cliché because I'd never seen him before and assumed he was a visitor. He really should not have had to put me straight. It was embarrassing for both of us.

The Head of Maths was a man named Ron Pedder. Nick met him at a music evening class in the autumn term of my second year at Creekside Comp. Naturally, upon hearing what Mr Pedder did and where, Nick said that his wife taught there too. I wasn't a bit surprised that one of the school's departmental heads had never heard my name and had no idea who I was.

One of the maths teachers who worked alongside me in Lower School was a jolly young man a year or two older than me and surprisingly skilled at taming boys with sums. He came from Sheffield and loved to thicken his accent to tease Mrs Port about 'mashing the tea'. On one of his rare visits to Lower School Ron Pedder was heard to ask with snobbish disdain, 'Who on earth is that terrible, loud man?'

Geoff couldn't resist it. 'One of your department, Ron, and a good teacher,' he said without a flicker. Even then I'm not sure the thick-skinned Pedder took the point or cared about it. And, sadly, his attitude was typical of a lot of the men who worked in Upper School.

As the anniversary of my original 'interview' with Mr Baker approached so did the end of the summer term, bringing with it all the delights of exams, reports and sports day – my first round of many of them.

I was told that I had to set and mark an end-of-year exam paper for each of the classes I taught. It might have made more sense for papers to be set across years but, perhaps because of the rigid streaming, that wasn't the way it was done at Creekside Comp.

Much of my English teaching was based – and continued to be so for the rest of my career – on a strong comprehension passage as a starting point. So I looked for some suitable passages outside the textbooks such as *The Art of English* and used these as the mainstay of each exam paper. I followed each one with some other work such as punctuation exercises and some composition or 'creative writing' titles.

I also had to come up with history and geography papers to cover the work I'd been doing with 1B.

Naturally, no one gave me any help or guidance with any of this. Having never before set, or even thought about how one might set, an exam paper, I had to make it up from scratch. As usual I simply remembered what had happened in my grammar school and came up with a version of it. I don't think anyone at college ever mentioned anything as practical and ordinary as routine summer exams.

The deal was that once you'd prepared your papers – in good time to a deadline – Janet and Margaret would type and duplicate them on the old-fashioned Gestetner machine. It meant that your exam papers looked quite professional for 1969 and it felt rather grown up. This was an exams-only service. Obviously Janet and Margaret wouldn't have had time to type everyone's resources throughout the year.

Tutor groups then did all their exams in their own classrooms with their own teacher in a single week with normal timetable suspended. It meant I had a very peaceful five days sitting with 1B while they scratched away at maths, science, English and all the rest of it. Afterwards it was simply a matter of handing the scripts to the teacher who had set them.

Then came the marking. And I had no idea just how long it would take. My papers were fiddly so that they were time consuming to mark and the totals awkward to calculate.

That was down to inexperienced setting. I hadn't even worked out that there are very good reasons for making sure that the maximum marks total 100 so that you don't have to convert to a percentage at the end. It is also sensible to keep marks for individual sections in units of 10 rather than indulging in fanciful figures such as 17 or 24.

I hadn't realised what an age it takes – especially if you've never done it before – to read answers and work out what they're worth. And of course the nature of exam answers is that they're samey and boring.

In short, I loathed it. And I went on hating exam marking for the rest of my teaching career. When I finally left the chalkface in 2004 people said I would miss it. Well, I certainly miss the students (as we call them these days) but there are plenty of things I don't miss at all and exam marking is top of the list.

For the reports we had to provide two marks. The first was for the exam and the second was a percentage for 'term work'. Now insofar as Creekside Comp had anything remotely resembling an 'assessment policy', it was that each individual piece of work was marked out of ten.

That meant that by the end of the year, if you were reasonably conscientious and had marked, say, one piece of work per boy per week, you had a mark book with more than thirty marks. The only way to get a percentage was to add them all up and do a calculation.

'Do you know how to do a percentage?' the bemused junior art teacher asked me earnestly one day when I was alone in the staffroom one day, his unmathematical eyes glazing in puzzlement. Well, yes I did and do. I'm no mathematician and had to take O Level maths twice but arithmetic was drilled into me at primary school. So I explained how you had to add all the marks together and put the total over your maximum before multiplying the fraction by 100 over 1.

But, if you taught as many pupils for as many subjects as I did all these sums would be hours of work, given that pocket calculators, such as they were, were crude, expensive and not yet commonplace. Where on earth was I to find that sort of time?

'Give your mark book to Grandpa, ask him to do it for you,' advised my father. 'He'll be really pleased to help. You see.'

My grandfather was by now visibly fading, although he still drove, went out every day, did his bit in the family business and marvelled at the moon landings which transfixed us all that summer. But he was developing that transparent look which cancer sufferers get in their last months. I've seen it many times since, although I didn't fully recognise it that first time.

But there was nothing wrong with him mentally, and he'd always been a whizz with figures, although his several throat cancer operations meant he could no longer speak normally. My father was right, as usual.

As a lifelong teacher himself, and very proud of me for carrying on the tradition, Grandfather was delighted to be involved and to feel useful. So it was the perfect solution and within a couple of days I had my two sets of marks for each class ready to put on the boys' reports.

Report writing was a novelty. Only four years earlier teachers had been writing things about me such as 'Susan is careless' or 'Could do better if she tried harder' or this one I particularly treasure from a teacher who clearly didn't know me at all – or perhaps it was late at night and she'd got me confused with someone else: 'Susan would write better if she read more.'

Now it was my turn to do the commenting. There was no guidance and some of the staff were very damning and negative: 'This boy is useless at maths' or 'Has no ability in this subject.'

Bearing in mind that these boys were all eleven plus failures and in need of support I tried, especially with first years, to be constructive, but subject comments were expected to be very brief so there wasn't much scope to do anything very useful.

Then, when the reports were complete, I had to write a fuller form teacher's summary comment – a short paragraph – to complete each 1B report. That was more satisfying and satisfactory because I knew those boys really well as individuals. It meant I could say something which I hoped was helpful, both to reassure them (in most cases) and their parents that the boy was working hard and making progress and to suggest ways of building on his achievement.

Also in the summer term we held parents' evenings – a daunting prospect for a novice. We sat at desks in the school library and parents came and talked to us. There was no appointment system so you had no idea what to expect. I was very nervous before my first one.

In fact, it panned out exactly as my wise father said it would. He said that only supportive parents of well-balanced, hard-working boys would turn up and that, as a teacher, you never see the parents of the awkward pupils you could do with putting straight. I don't think that was always entirely the case later in my career but it was certainly the pattern at Creekside Comp.

I met only charming, caring parents, most of whom told me how pleased they were with the work I was doing with their sons who, they assured me, enjoyed coming to school. They spoke very positively about me too. And some of them were alarmingly deferential considering how little I really knew about anything. I noticed especially that West Indian parents had been brought up to venerate and respect teachers, and that rather disconcerting (to me, at any rate) attitude was still with them.

Much relieved, I repaired afterwards to The Duke over the road with Geoff and Jack Rowlands – as we were always to do after parents' meetings. The Duke is the only building in this story which is still standing and doing exactly what it always did. Except that it used to be a perfectly ordinary pint-and-a-packet-of-crisps wooden-floored Deptford pub. It is now a rather chi-chi gastropub meeting the needs, presumably, of the many well-paid flat dwellers who live nearby because it's so handy for Docklands and the City.

Back then The Duke was just our local. We sometimes popped over at lunchtime and invariably at the end of term or if, for any reason, we were on school premises during holidays. The liver sausage sandwiches – this was some years before I became a vegetarian – were especially good.

Soon it was time for Lower School Sports Day, which was held in Deptford Park, about a mile along Evelyn Street. The boys were supposed to walk there in their tutor groups accompanied by their teacher.

Well, I managed to get the biddable 1B there intact, but for colleagues with second- and third-year classes the trick was to lose all the potential troublemakers along the way. The boys who just saw it as the perfect opportunity to truant, sometimes with teacher connivance, or at least a blind eye, would melt away too. Geoff, for example, had only a handful of 3F in tow when he arrived at the park and regarded that as a success.

Once there the PE men had track events and so on organised and we were all supposed to sit and watch. As far as I was concerned the whole event was a dreadful bore. Geoff, who felt the same way, and I just sat there and gossiped. I've never had the slightest interest in competitive sports and hated school sports days from then on, almost as much as I disliked exam marking.

Because I'd now been teaching for a year, it was time for me to be assessed to see whether I'd completed my probationary year successfully. Today this is quite a formal process towards 'Qualified Teacher Status' and the word 'probationary' doesn't come into it. In 1969 it was casual in the extreme and 'assess' was something of an overstatement.

I hadn't killed, injured or molested any boys – at least not as far as anyone knew. I seemed to be able to keep most of the boys in my classroom most of the time – without too much noise, at least if the door was shut. I usually turned up and tried to do what I was paid to do. So I was clearly going to 'pass' with flying colours.

The formal bit involved Mr Baker arriving one day in my classroom and sitting in on a 1B lesson for about ten minutes. I think it was the only time I had another adult in the classroom during the whole year. Then he bumbled off.

A week or two later, I had a letter from ILEA confirming that the formalities were complete and that I was now a fully fledged teacher.

Meanwhile at home Nick and I had decided that we were ready to become a feline family. We had both grown up with cats and felt that a kitten would complete our home. The flat, with its little garden, was more than suitable. So where were we to get one?

I mentioned to 1B one day that we were in the market for a kitten and Mark Shaw piped up. He had a friend from primary school, with whom he still played cricket, whose cat had had a litter. Would I like him to make enquiries?

Mark and his mother arranged for me to call at the home of the other family early one evening and Mark was there to perform the introductions.

Mark's friend Raj was clearly very bright and articulate. His parents were both doctors. Raj had inevitably sailed into a grammar school and the meeting brought home to me just how difficult gentle Mark and other boys like him must find life at Creekside Comp when their contemporaries were having such a very different experience elsewhere.

Lovely people, Raj's family made me very welcome and it was a pleasure to see Mark in an out-of-school setting. We all had refreshments and a good chat. Then I went home with an exquisitely marked tabby kitten we called Claud.

Term finally ended and the summer holidays stretched enticingly ahead with plenty of time to acclimatise Claud to living with us.

We couldn't afford to go anywhere much because we'd had a week in Paris after our wedding in the spring. Instead we hired a pretty indifferent caravan near Beddgelert at the foot of Snowdon for a week. We took Claud with us and he spent most of the week running away from two beautiful, but boisterous, Dalmatians named Bramble and Pippin who were staying in the next-door caravan.

Somehow we managed to get our precious feline dependant home in one piece. Then it was back to school for my second year.

CHAPTER EIGHT

New school years always mean changes and September 1969 was no exception. Although I still had 1B – now 2B – as my tutor group, I also acquired new classes, including a couple of first-year groups.

3F had gone off – or at least the non-truanting ones had – to make a nuisance of themselves as 4F in Upper School and I found my 'new' third-year group marginally – but no more than that – easier because I'd known them as second years, the year before. At least they knew I'd got staying power.

There is also a lot to be said for not being new. Only the third years now remembered a time when I wasn't there and to the new first years I could pretend to be an old hand.

I felt more secure having been right through the whole process once too. I could, for example, revisit the same work with my new first-year English classes that I'd already done with the previous 1A and 1B. And I could re-use the comprehension cards with my lower-ability second-year class because I knew they worked. And increased confidence is never a hindrance in teaching.

Now aware that I would eventually have to produce class marks at the end of the year, I organised my mark book to make it simpler. Running totals were the common sense solution. It was still far from easy but the second year was definitely better than the first.

Some staff had moved on too, so there were new arrivals or, at least, rumours of them. The new timetable, which as usual we didn't get until the first morning of term, featured a Mr Godinton who had been working in France and was coming to do some French and other teaching, partly because Heloise was having a baby and was due to begin her maternity leave before Christmas.

The problem was that he wasn't there. 'There's been a delay. He'll be here any day now,' was the vague message which came out of Upper School and from Mr Baker when he was pressed.

Meanwhile we had to cover those lessons. The non-appearance of Mr Godinton – dubbed by Geoff as 'Waiting for Godot' – soon became a bitter joke as we toiled on. He never did turn up and we were left wondering whether he'd been a figment of headmasterly imagination or perhaps Godot had had a better offer. In the end the timetable had to be rewritten.

Bruce West, however, appeared on day one. He was divisional staff like me but he'd already taught for a year or two. It didn't occur to me to wonder why, in that case, he hadn't by now been permanently assigned to a school.

He was young, slim with fair curly hair and had that libertarian, anarchic 'progressive', often flawed, 1960s determination about him. Bruce immediately allied himself with Tom Reece who'd arrived when I started the year before.

Tom was around twenty-five and had come to Creekside Comp as assigned staff to run the Lower School library for which he had a 'Scale 2' post. He had a wan face, wore his hippy-long hair tied back in a ponytail and played the guitar.

He and Bruce – with me – were responsible for first-year history and geography teaching and they wanted to create an integrated humanities project with the three of us team teaching. It sounds a good and reasonable idea now but at the time it was a step much too far for those boys who were just about manageable with a lot of up-front structure and a lost cause without it.

It also has to be said that I was still very inexperienced and neither Bruce nor Tom had any real aptitude for this way of working. It may look casual but it is supposed to be anything but. In our case it both looked, and was, casual in the extreme.

We were timetabled for a whole afternoon of humanities because Tom had made a good case when the timetable was being created. And we had block topics, one of which was the Wild West – cue for Tom to play his guitar and for Bruce and me to enjoy ourselves singing along, but I don't think it taught the boys anything much.

Then in our classrooms we had to do this Wild West stuff about which I knew almost nothing, although I made valiant efforts to learn what chaps, corrals, Stetsons and so on are. There were worksheets and tasks. And the boys had to do creative writing based on woefully sketchy information. There was very little substance or rigour in any of it.

I doubt that Tom and Bruce were sensitive to the vibes but I could clearly feel the hostility from the rest of the staff and what appeared to them to be a self-indulgent cop out by two 'lefty' young men. With every succeeding week I became increasingly bored, disenchanted and utterly convinced that – although my misguided teacher training college would undoubtedly have approved of it – this wasn't proper teaching and learning.

The project died at the end of the year, unlamented by me and others, when Tom left the school for a job in a 'progressive' independent school. He told me once, on a visit to Creekside, that he now taught pupils such as the son of actor Albert Finney. Let's hope they were more suited to his academically questionable, guitar-strumming ways than 1960s Deptford boys were.

The biggest and most difficult thing I had to cope with that term was personal, not professional. My beloved grandfather died early in the morning of Tuesday 23 September. It was the first death of anyone close to me and it was deeply traumatic.

He died at home having collapsed in the bedroom and haemorrhaged to death on the carpet while my hysterical, distraught grandmother tried in vain to call a doctor. So there was nothing peaceful or well managed about his death and we were all, especially my poor grandmother, devastated.

I had a very special relationship with my grandparents who'd been a very strong force in my life for as long as I could remember. After the war my parents, in common with so many of their generation, had nowhere to live, so when I was a pre-schooler we lodged for nearly three years with Grandpa and Grandma. He was teaching round the corner in the primary school I would attend from age five, and she looked after me while my parents were at work.

When my parents found somewhere of their own to live it was a flat over a shop 200 yards along the road from the grandparental home. The idea was that they would run their own business on those premises, which they did pretty successfully in partnership with my unmarried uncle who still lived with his parents. Eventually there was a second shop and my grandparents were active participants in the business from the day my parents started it until the death of my grandmother in 1987.

Although my grandparents downsized and moved out to West Wickham while I was in the sixth form, and we moved into a house near the main shop when I was thirteen, I saw my grandparents almost every day until I went to college at age eighteen.

Grandpa's death hit me like a sledgehammer. On the day that he died, I got the phone call at about 7am. I had a full timetable that morning so I went to school and, somehow, stumbled numbly through those lessons. I had some 'free' periods in the afternoon, so Jack Rowlands kindly gave me leave to go and sit with my grandmother in my parents' house. She was still hysterical. I found it very difficult to help her without caving in myself but at least my being there meant that my parents could have a few minutes' respite to begin to deal with their own grief.

Grandpa's funeral – for which I had a whole day off – was held on the Friday of that week in the church next to our flat where he had been, for many years through the 1950s and early '60s, churchwarden, fundraiser and many other things.

As I write this I am facing a small memorial plaque and an exquisite back-lit little stained glass window which looks glorious in an alcove in our dining room. The church people raised the money for this window after my grandfather's death and it was placed near the main door. When I heard, in the 1990s, that the long-since deconsecrated church was to be converted to flats, I managed to acquire the window and give it a safe home. The plaque reads, 'In grateful memory of William C.H. Hillyer born 21st July 1896, died 23rd September 1969. May he rest in peace.'

I'm glad he lived long enough to see me, his eldest grandchild, happily married and holding my own as a teacher. Alas, dead at seventy-three, he didn't even know all his grandchildren and never saw any of his great grandchildren – eleven at the last count.

At school Mr Baker announced that he would be retiring at Easter. It didn't take me by surprise, particularly because he really did seem very old to me and had, as he was fond of reminding everyone, been teaching in Deptford since 1930. His presence – actually mostly absence from Lower School – didn't impinge on me very much, anyway. But it obviously meant that major changes were likely to be afoot before too long and there was a lot of staffroom speculation about the future.

Jack Rowlands and Geoff, meanwhile, were hatching a plan. I overheard them talking about a residential trip to France which would run later that school year. I knew they'd taken several trips together in the past because Geoff had told me about them.

Geoff was, at that time, the only person I'd ever met who had been to Russia. Because of his communist leanings, he was fascinated by the Soviet way of life and had twice led school trips to Moscow and Leningrad (as St Petersburg was then known), although he'd done it with other staff rather than Jack Rowlands who'd been at the school for only three or four years.

Given the visa and other complications of taking thirty teenagers behind the Iron Curtain into Khrushchev country, it was an extraordinarily enterprising thing to do at that time.

Not that Geoff was much of a traveller. Apart from the school trips he did in the 1950s and '60s, Geoff never ventured abroad in the entire forty years I knew him. He wouldn't even take Coral to Venice to see the art. All he really wanted to do for holidays normally was to chug along British Waterways first on a friend's, and later his own, boat.

Anyway here he was, in 1969, planning a trip for boys from all age groups to the French Alps and Lakes in July 1970 with Jack Rowlands. 'Oh, are you going to France? That's sounds nice,' I said casually, really without any thought. 'Yes, Heloise is coming – she'll have had her baby by then. Do you want to come too?' they asked.

It seemed like a spur of the moment invitation but surely they must have thought about it in advance and had been waiting for the right moment to suggest it? After all, it's important on a ten-day residential trip to be sure you've got colleagues who can work together, relate to the pupils and not rub each other up the wrong way. They must have discussed it before they mentioned it in front of me.

'Yes please,' I said. And from then on the trip to Annecy and Paris was something to look forward to and plan. Quite by chance I had started an evening class in French at Goldsmiths College at the beginning of the school year.

My French had been pretty good after O Level and during several long stays in French families, so I was keen to practise my newly brushed-up skills and this trip looked like a good opportunity. Months later, while we were away, Heloise heard me say, *'Parce que j'ai cru…'* to a French coach driver and congratulated me for knowing the correct past participle of the irregular verb *croire* (to believe), so my efforts must have paid off.

But we had to get through two more school terms before that. And staffing problems were as acute as ever.

From time to time a 'supply' teacher would appear to help us all out. Now, the truth then was – although it's different now –

that any half-decent teacher who wanted a job could get one. The bar was pretty low.

It was axiomatic, therefore, that almost anyone who holed up as a supply teacher was likely to be flawed. And that applied especially to men because they were unlikely at that time to have childcare responsibility. There were women, although we never saw one at Creekside Comp, who opted to do supply work as a way of getting flexible, part-time work while their children were young. But it was different for men.

And we had a whole succession of them. Geoff maintained, with that wicked twinkle and imagination which was the only thing that kept him sane for all those years in that environment, that every head had a trapdoor in his office. Out of said hole, like the apparitions in *Macbeth*, said Geoff, would pop the flotsam and jetsam of the teaching profession to be shoved straight out of the head's door and into the classrooms of the school.

Not that they were supply teachers in the accepted sense. Never in all the years I was at Creekside Comp did we see a fill-in teacher hired for the day because someone had phoned in sick. No, these strange men were brought in as full-time teachers because we never had enough staff on the payroll to cover the timetable. They differed from the rest of us only in that they were loosely temporary, so could disappear at the drop of a hat, and I don't think they'd been sent from Divisional Office.

One such was Mr Tufnell, whose given name was never revealed or discovered. His habit – we quickly realised he was virtually homeless and mentally very unwell – was to arrive in Deptford at 5.30am. He would then get breakfast in one of the greasy spoon cafés in the High Street which opened early. After that he'd kick his heels around Deptford for an hour or two and come into school as soon as the caretaker opened the doors for staff about 7.30. So when Geoff and I arrived, and we were usually among the first, Mr Tufnell would already be sitting in the staffroom gazing inscrutably and uncomfortably into the distance. I never saw him smile.

He hardly spoke and was, inevitably, a disaster in the classroom where the boys either ignored or ridiculed him.

Geoff, ever good at drawing people out and actually quite kind, managed on one occasion, when he and Mr Tufnell were alone in the staffroom, to have a chat with him. 'My marriage broke up because of William Tell,' he told Geoff lugubriously.

'William Tell?' returned the astonished Geoff incredulously, trying not to shout.

'You see, I'm an opera lover and I can't sleep so I used to play my operas on the gramophone downstairs nice and loud. One night when I put *William Tell* on at about midnight to run through the night my wife appeared and said she was taking the children to her mother's and not coming back.'

Geoff and I laughed about it but Mr Tufnell was clearly really a sad case and in need of a lot of help. Unsurprisingly – even I could see at a glance that he was not likely to be much use as a teacher – he did nothing to ease our staffing problems. After a few weeks we saw him no more.

Mr de la Touche, another one whose given name I never discovered, was a silent, stylish ebony-skinned man who always wore very smart three-piece suits. I suppose his family must originally have hailed from one of the French colonies, hence the French name.

He was a strict disciplinarian who actually got the boys working pretty hard in a traditional, almost Victorian, way and they were wary of him. Mr de la Touche had beautiful and perfectly formed handwriting, which it always seemed a shame to rub off the board if you went into a room to teach after him.

His first problem was that he didn't relate to anyone else. He spoke neither to staff nor boys except to shoot instructions at the latter. The second thing was his attendance. He was meant to be at Creekside Comp full-time but we rarely saw him more than twice or three times a week. Jack Rowlands was convinced that Mr de la Touche had another job somewhere and was drawing full salaries for both. I once saw him coming out of a betting shop in Forest Hill.

Mr Gupta, a maths teacher, was a turban-wearing Sikh, which made him, at that time, one novelty too many for most of the boys.

Although it makes me cringe now to think of it, there was a Sikh boy in the new first year called Merry (or at least that's the name he was known by) Khatri. He had been brought to his interview with his hair tied up in the traditional pre-adolescent, covered Sikh topknot. Jack Rowlands had told the parents bluntly that they'd have to get Merry's hair cut if they wanted him to be accepted by the other boys. Almost unbelievably, the parents – eager for their boy to do well, I suppose – had done just that.

Well, with that racist attitude pragmatically condoned in the school by senior staff, there was precious little hope for Mr Gupta. He was very quickly seen off by gleeful, whooping boys as soon as they realised he was gentle – or weak, as it would have seemed to them. His Indian accent with its un-English stresses was, by Deptford standards, pretty impenetrable too.

I once had quite a long conversation with Mr Gupta. He travelled in each day from Essex, which must have been a dreadful journey and a sure sign that he was having great difficulty getting work. He lived with his extended family including parents, cousins and others as they would have done in India. Mr Gupta had recently suffered appendicitis, which his wife treated with balm before they realised that he really would have to go to the hospital. It was all a long way from what most Deptford boys felt at home with.

Occasionally a really good teacher popped out of the trapdoor. We were privileged, and so were the boys, to have Joe Smith for two terms, He was an Australian with a good degree and teaching qualifications from an Australian university. He'd taught there for a couple of years. Now he and his wife, also a teacher, were working their way round Europe before – I imagine – going home to settle down and start a family.

Joe taught maths and PE, had natural authority and teaching ability and was liked and respected by everyone he came into contact with. We were all sorry to see him go when the time came for him to move on. No doubt he went on to a good career and a headmastership in Australia – with Creekside Comp as one of the less conventional experiences listed on his CV.

Easter came and Mr Baker went with all the usual send-offs, gifts and eulogies associated with the retirement of heads.

Our new 'Old Man' was not due to start until September so we had a term's interregnum under Mr Greening, who had been Mr Baker's deputy. The change made no difference whatever to me. I'd never spoken to Mr Greening before he took over as Acting Head and I'm pretty sure I never did during the term of his 'reign'. He was just someone I saw – very occasionally – in the distance as you might the Duke of Edinburgh if he visited your town.

And at the end of term he was going off to take up a permanent headship elsewhere.

Creekside Comp was an unaccountably good springboard for ambitious people who wanted to go on to higher things. The Head of History left that term to become curator of a major London museum, only to be one of the earliest AIDS deaths a few years later. Jack Rowlands later went on to a headship too and there were others.

As the end of term approached so did the ten-day trip to Paris and Annecy. Jack Rowlands was the party leader, ably assisted by Geoff. They did all the preparation and I don't recall being asked to do anything to help. I really seemed to be going along just for the ride. And with hindsight, of course, I now realise that neither Jack nor Geoff minded in the least spending ten days in the company of a twenty-three-year-old woman with legs and long hair. It made the enterprise seem less monastic.

We were taking a group of about thirty boys from across all years, including three sixth formers, whom I didn't know at all but

Jack and Geoff did. Most were from the first, second and third years, so they were lads I saw every day, including Merry Khatri.

We left on 14 July a few days before the end of term, taking the train from Waterloo to Dover and then another train through northern France to Gare du Nord – which took most of the day. We were then due to get the night train from Gare de Lyon, leaving about midnight. It meant a long evening of hanging about but I'd been quite looking forward to it because I thought it might be fun to be in Paris on the evening of Bastille Day.

In the event it was a cold, wet, damp squib and if there were any celebrations and parties in Paris that night they passed me by completely. We ate a pre-booked meal near Gare de Lyon and then Jack, Geoff and I based ourselves in an indifferent café near the station for the evening. Jack sent the boys off in groups to be rained on, supervised by the sixth formers with instructions that they had to report back to him every hour. Oh those balmy, irresponsible days before the invention of risk assessments!

Heloise was not with us at this point. She was staying with her parents in Dijon. She would leave her baby with them and join us on the train south at around 2.30am.

The evening wore on slowly until it was time to convene at the station and board the train. I was pretty tired by then, having now been travelling for fourteen hours, and in those days I could sleep like a kitten. No chance on this occasion. Our full second-class carriage was hard and uncomfortable in a way that only a 1970s French train could be. I spend the night bolt upright, wide awake and unable to move my feet more than an inch or two wedged between Geoff and the window facing a row of boys, all of whom snuffed out like candles and slept soundly until we reached Annecy six or more hours later.

At Dijon we duly acquired Heloise as arranged. How she felt able to 'abandon' her child, who was under six months, for over a week I'll never understand and I think Jack and Geoff, both fathers with wives, were a bit puzzled by it too. The baby was at Dijon station with Heloise's parents to see her off – also a bit odd considering the uncivilised hour of day/night. She was slightly weepy as the train pulled out and a bit quiet once or twice during the week in Annecy. Otherwise it was business as usual for the professional Mrs Scott who, as a native French speaker, was obviously a key member of the party.

The accommodation in Annecy was a huge, old-fashioned *lycée* with boarding facilities. The boys slept in a vast dormitory, easily the size of the average secondary school hall, with a stark row of beds down either side. At the door end was a basic twin-bedded room with a window overlooking the dormitory – term-time accommodation for *les moniteurs*, Heloise explained – and this was where Jack and Geoff were to sleep. Christophe Barratier's 2004 film, *Les Choristes*, shows an almost identical set-up.

Heloise and I were assigned a twin room with a typically French plug-free wash basin about half a mile of corridor away – presumably to keep us well away from males, some of whom were, no doubt, a bit turned on at the thought of the two of us undressed on the same premises.

On the first morning I just fell into bed, only to be roused by Geoff a couple of hours later for lunch in the *lycée* followed by a stroll round Annecy – a chocolate box town with lots of water, bridges and flowers.

Heloise really was a French woman to her core. In the seven days that she and I slept in that room I never saw her undress or perform any ablutions beyond washing her face and hands. I, on the other hand, probably outraged her Gallic 'modesty' by insisting, in my English way, on stripping off and washing all over because there was no shower anywhere near our room.

I also did a deal with Jack and Geoff. I would be the party's alarm clock. Each morning I crept out of bed early and trudged through the corridors in my dressing gown carrying my wash bag. On arrival at the boys' department, I would wake Jack and Geoff, who would then supervise the dormitory via their open door and prevent any boy from coming into the attached shower block while I showered. Then I traipsed back to the room I shared with Heloise to dress while Jack and Geoff got the boys up.

We had excursions planned through the week because we were on a package arranged by a company specialising in school trips. We visited, for example, Mer de Glace, the famous glacier near Chamonix. There was a very interesting dam which provided hydro-electric power for much of the region and a coach trip round Lake Chambery which Jack Rowlands aborted because he decided that the driver was endangering the lives of his passengers – so health and safety was a consideration after all.

We had good, but basic, breakfasts and dinners in the *lycée* and were issued with packed lunches. In the evenings two of us would go out for a drink while the other two babysat. Inevitably I teamed up with Geoff and Heloise with Jack.

One day Merry, released from central supervision for an hour or two, went shoplifting. He was caught and Heloise used all her diplomatic skills to dissuade the shop from taking matters any further. But Merry had to be punished – and, perhaps, made an example of.

So Jack Rowlands took him away to a private room and caned him. Yes, caned him. Had he taken a cane with him in case he needed it? Did he improvise? Even at the time – when caning was an almost daily occurrence at Creekside Comp – it seemed to me a desperately inappropriate thing to do when we were all bonding together and establishing a rather different sort of out-of-school relationship with each other. The strange thing was that Merry's being caned didn't seem to affect that. He was his normal cheerful self the next day and the matter wasn't mentioned again.

It was all quite enjoyable and interesting but I was pretty homesick. It was the longest I'd been away from Nick since we'd become a couple over four years earlier and it felt very strange. Fortunately the post was very fast and reliable in those pre-email and mobile phone days, so we wrote to each other several times.

At the end of the week the party returned by train to Paris, leaving Heloise at Dijon. Then came three nights in a rather different city centre *lycée* in Paris – where I was assigned a curtained cubicle in a dormitory on my own like a deserted hospital ward. It felt uneasily inappropriate when Geoff popped round in the mornings to check I was awake, and I tried to be up and dressed before he arrived.

Coach trips round the main sights took in La Tour Eiffel, Notre Dame and Le Château de Versailles before it was time to head home via Gare du Nord.

Nick met me at Waterloo sporting a surprise new moustache which I liked, so he has had it ever since – although, sadly, it is no longer the brown it was in 1970.

He also had a surprise for me at home. We'd had it in mind for a while to get another cat to keep Claud company. A client of my social worker mother-in-law had a litter so, back at the flat, I was introduced to a very pretty female tortoiseshell kitten we named Emily.

But there was, almost literally, a sting in the tail. Nick hadn't seen Claud since the previous day and was very worried. The day after I got back from France we found Claud dead in the long grass at the front of the flats. He'd been hit by a car. Of course it must have been coincidence, but neither of us could ever get the idea out of our heads that Claud had felt usurped by Emily and gone off and run in front of a car almost deliberately. We felt very sad and it put a damper on my homecoming. And, poor beast, Emily became the least loved of all the cats we've ever had, although in due course she presented us with a lovely litter of five kittens, one of which we kept when we found homes for the others.

Term had ended during the French trip. And my third year – with a new and very different sort of headmaster – lay ahead.

CHAPTER NINE

Cedric Flyte was quite something. A bespectacled man in his fifties he was short of stature, although so big and forceful in personality that you didn't notice his stocky height until you stood next to him.

He'd had a successful headship at another South London school in a 'difficult' area and had obviously been persuaded – in return for a huge pension-enhancing salary, I suspect – by ILEA bigwigs to take on Creekside Comp. We certainly ticked all the boxes for being a school in trouble. Today it would be in Ofsted-ian 'special measures' (or worse) and Cedric would be dubbed a 'superhead' mounted on the headmasterly equivalent of a white charger with the 7th Cavalry of the education army behind him.

Actually he arrived in a flamboyant bright green MG sports car with a personalised number plate. He was the first person I knew personally to indulge in such extravagant egotism. He changed his car annually. Next there came a white Triumph Stag. Each car was more showy than the last. Freudian undertones, perhaps. He was, after all, physically a short man.

And as for his name. Well, I suppose it wasn't his fault that his parents had landed him with that unusual and faintly comic forename to add to their monosyllabic surname. From the start everyone addressed him as 'Mr Flyte' to his face but always referred to him as 'Cedric' in the third person behind his back because it seemed such an unlikely name. It wasn't long before the boys were mockingly murmuring, mouthing or squealing 'Cedric' when he passed, as long as they were sure he wouldn't be able to identify or catch them.

He couldn't help being named like something out of a Dickens novel, but he could have avoided the bumptiousness which sometimes made him a laughing stock – a dangerous position for someone who has a lot to prove as a 'superhead' in a school which offered rather more challenges than strengths. In time he told a handful of senior staff – one of whom was Geoff, which is how I came to know about it – 'Call me "Cedric" but not in front of the staff.' That was fairly typical of his mind-your-back management style.

When he spoke to me, as to his credit he quite often did, he called me 'Susan' in the patronising way which used to be the norm for heads striking a balance between avuncular kindness and keeping a distance.

Cedric's wife was something very senior in BBC production and between them they had many useful, high-profile contacts, some of whom appeared at the school from time to time. Lady Plowden, author of the famous 1967 Plowden Report, 'Children and their Primary Schools', came informally, for instance, and I found myself chatting to her over school lunch. We also had visits from the top political names of the day such as Anthony Crosland and Edward Short, among others.

When Cedric first came to Creekside Comp, he and Mrs Flyte lived a couple of miles away in the suburb where he'd had his first headship. Now, presumably on the strength of his new fat salary (and he always said that his wife was the main household earner, so between them they must have been bringing in quite an income) they decided to move out of town.

They bought a house in a village in North Kent, an hour's drive away, which seemed a pretty daft thing to do given that they both worked in London. Or perhaps it was to make sure that those flashy cars had plenty of work to do. Driving home late one night he was stopped on the M2 doing 103 mph. 'Do you know how fast you were going, sir?' asked the police officer sternly. 'No. When you're driving as fast as I was it's best to keep your eyes on the road,' replied Cedric – according to Geoff, at least. Goodness knows what Cedric had to pay for motor insurance.

Some time later Geoff attended senior staff meetings in Cedric's Kent home and reported that it was like a Hollywood set. 'It looks huge from outside – very long and thin and showy – but it's only one room deep so actually not all that large,' he reported, unable to resist the quip that Cedric had bought a house which reflected his personality. All noise, bluster and appearance without much substance.

The house was, I suppose, a sort of upmarket downsizing with a view to eventual retirement. The three Flyte children had all flown the nest and, by the time I met Cedric, there were several grandchildren.

The first big change from any head or quasi-head we'd had before was that Cedric was present – in person. The little green monster graced our playground all day long. From day one he spent almost all his time in Lower School. And he tried to run it. His big mission was, it quickly became apparent, to unify the split-site school and he evidently thought that a bottom-up approach was the way forward.

But first he had to deal with the Fire Bell Problem. Ever since I'd been at the school it had been a game for boys to smash the glass on one of the alarm signals several times a week. If you were a boy with a grudge, or who was bored, or out for a laugh, it was an activity which paid splendid dividends in terms of maximum fuss and disruption. Strident electric bells resonated at conversation-drowning pitch in every corner of the building. And the entire school had to stop what it was doing immediately and troop out into the playground – including shivering skinny boys in PE vests, Pete Sargeant's lads in their workshop aprons and the irritated kitchen staff in their snowy white overalls and hats. And if it was snowing, raining or blowing a howling gale then so much the better for the pranksters – whose identity no one could ever ascertain or prove.

We went through this charade so often that it was very difficult even for responsible adults to take these continual fire alarms seriously. On one occasion in my second year, before Cedric's arrival, I was sitting marking books alone in my classroom when the fire alarm sounded. I swore to myself and, for the first and only time ever, decided to ignore it. I knew it was only yet another puerile prank and I wanted to get those books marked before the end of the period. I also knew, or thought I did, that because this was yet another hoax, checking would be perfunctory and no one would miss me.

After a few minutes I heard a fire engine come up Creek Road with its claxon going. I took no notice because there was nothing especially unusual about that on a busy main road. Then there was another one. And suddenly I twigged: 'Bloody hell! Fire engines, Fire Bell!' I don't think I've ever moved so fast.

When I opened the door of my room it was to see Ian Ellis, Jack Rowlands and others, grim-faced and shepherding hundreds of boys to the staircases at either end of the building. I snapped into action and helped to evacuate the school feeling deeply ashamed, with phrases such as 'dereliction of duty' and *in loco parentis* rattling about in my head.

Later I found out that three truants from lessons had been smoking in the big cupboard under the main staircase where some old camping equipment was stored. A smouldering butt left in the cupboard had ignited the contents and a pretty serious fire had taken hold before anyone noticed. The central staircase obviously couldn't be used during the emergency, leaving the whole school with just two, instead of three, evacuation routes. The fire officers soon got it under control but one of them described it as an inferno.

By golly, was that a lesson for me. However many false alarms there may have been you must never, ever, ignore a fire alarm. I think I told the story – against myself as a warning – of the day

I didn't bother to every class I taught for the rest of my teaching career. And for ever after, woe betide anyone I was responsible for who took fire alarms and drills less than seriously.

On the other hand you need only heed fire bells if they are the standard way of raising the alarm. The problem of false alarms had become so disruptive in pre-Cedric days that Jack Rowlands and the people who worked most closely with us had issued different instructions and been pretty scrupulous about making sure that every member of staff knew about the new arrangements.

We were told that if the electric fire bell went we were to ignore it. If there was a real fire or other emergency – or Jack and co wanted to hold a routine fire drill – the hand bell would be rung. So that's what we did. It probably wasn't all that safe. But it worked more or less and at least it meant that lessons weren't wilfully disrupted almost every day.

I think it was on Cedric's second day that the electric fire alarm was set off by some boy or boys out for a giggle and wanting to see what happened. And of course, every man, woman and child on the premises ignored it.

To say Cedric was horrified would be a bit of an understatement. He was furious, livid, enraged, incredulous and appalled. Several hours later, when he summoned the staff at the end of the day, he was still spluttering with rage and indignation. And the harder we tried to tell him that ignoring the electric bell had been a policy decision and that we footsoldiers were merely following instructions, the crosser and more outraged he got.

In future, he instructed, we were to treat every sounding of the fire alarm as a *bona fide* serious emergency and evacuate the school immediately.

What followed was a real test of Cedric's strength. As soon as the boys realised there was a new policy they reverted to smashing the glass at every opportunity.

Cedric, clearly educated in the Caliguan School of Management, had his own way of finding the culprit. It was grossly unfair and unreasonable. A century earlier he'd probably have publicly beaten every tenth boy. What he did in 1970 was this.

If the fire alarm had been deliberately set off during the day, Cedric would assemble the entire school and staff in the yard when the last lesson, Period 8, ended. We had to escort them down to make sure no one escaped.

Of course there were no seats. The boys stood wearily in lines, supervised by form staff. Other teachers stood around in desultory huddles. Cedric strutted about at the front with a megaphone informing his school that no one was going anywhere until he got either a confession from the fire alarm glass smasher or information leading to identification of the culprit.

Sometimes we stood there for an hour until Cedric got what he wanted. It was always very tense and a real clash of wills. By rights it shouldn't have worked. In practice it always did – eventually. Usually someone would get so fed up with, and worn down by, the situation that he'd either confess or 'grass' on the culprit. Cedric, meanwhile, seemed completely unfazed by any concern for parents who might be expecting their children home or who were waiting for them at the gate. Not that many secondary school pupils were met from school in 1970 but some of the younger boys would have had mothers at home anxiously wondering where their kids had got to.

If challenged Cedric would have said that the end justified the means and that the boys had to be shown who was in charge. And, since within a couple of weeks false fire alarms had more or less stopped, I suppose he had a point, although I have never been comfortable with any policy which punishes everyone for the sins of an individual or tiny minority.

Meanwhile Cedric was asserting himself around school in other ways too. He announced at his first staff meeting that he had asked for a copy of everyone's timetable. Armed with these he would be visiting every teacher's classroom, unannounced, to observe a lesson at some point during that first term.

He arrived affably at my door at the beginning of a lesson with a first-year class just as I was seeing the boys in. He then sat at my desk at the front – no discreet observation from the back for Cedric who liked to be seen – while I taught the lesson standing between the old-fashioned roller blackboard and the front row of desks. He didn't interrupt or attempt to join in, he simply watched. It was the only time I was fully observed teaching in the whole five years I was at Creekside Comp.

He must have been reasonably happy with what he saw and heard in my classroom because he was kind and supportive to me for all the rest of the time I knew him. In fact, as we shall see, he went out of his way to be so.

It certainly wasn't like that for everyone and some of our 'characters' disappeared quickly and quietly early in Cedric's reign. I have no idea whether, for instance, Timmy Fletcher, the hapless musician, was sacked, pensioned off or eased back via Divisional Office to another school, but he didn't last more than a term or two of Cedric's headship. Pat McGuire was soon off the payroll too.

So was Bruce West, although that was for a different, very specific reason. Still teaching his own, apparently unsupervised, version of a vague integrated humanities curriculum, Bruce took a group of boys by coach to London Zoo. He must surely have had another member of staff with him but Bruce was in charge of the trip.

At the end of the day, he rounded up his charges and took them home to Deptford. He dismissed them at the school entrance and went home. The trouble was he hadn't done that most elementary thing which all teachers the world over do on school trips. He had failed to count heads before leaving the zoo.

So three boys – aged thirteen and fourteen – were left behind. They were, presumably, doing their own thing around the zoo and Regent's Park because it was several hours and quite late into the evening before they realised that they had been left behind and had no means of getting home. In the end they had to ask for help and the police got involved.

Somehow, the police – via the school caretaker perhaps – got Cedric's home number because, of course, these were Creekside Comp boys and therefore Cedric's ultimate responsibility. The police insisted that Cedric, who was fortunately still living in South London at that time, drive to Regent's Park to collect 'his' boys and take them home.

We never saw Bruce West again. He was still divisional staff, so Cedric had only to tell the Divisional Officer that he wanted this man removed and the deed was done. When I last heard of him he'd been sent to a school in Brockley where he was no doubt wreaking insouciant, anarchic havoc.

Fortunately I never lost any children at the zoo. In fact I led a trip all the way to Longleat in Wiltshire later that year and brought every boy back safely. The ability to count is quite an asset in teaching. So my face seemed to fit and it wasn't long before I got a summons to Cedric's office – now firmly established in our Lower School building.

He wanted to talk to me about two things. First he wanted to recommend that I become 'assigned' staff – which meant that I would be a fully fledged member of staff who couldn't be returned to Divisional Office like faulty goods, however many children I lost.

I have the official letter in front of me. It is dated 2 November 1970 and is signed by ILEA's Education Officer, Sir William Houghton – whose entry in the *New Oxford Dictionary of National Biography* I was, as chance has it, eventually to write. 'It is with pleasure I inform you that you have been assigned to Creekside (SB) School from 19th October,' wrote Sir William or one of his minions. 'Whenever you write to the Authority, will you kindly state that you are a teacher at this school.'

Of course I was delighted. It was the last stage in being recognised as a proper teacher in a permanent job.

The other thing Cedric wanted to discuss with me was a promotion. And I suppose that was why we had to deal with the assignment to the school first. Without that I wouldn't have been eligible for the promotion.

Tom Reece had left the school the previous term so the library was rudderless. Cedric wanted to know if I'd be willing to take on the school library. If so, he'd give me a 'point'. In those days assistant teachers – that is those who weren't heads or deputies – were paid on a points system according to the level of responsibility they carried. One point was the lowest level. Geoff had three for looking after Lower School science and goodness knows how many the remote heads of department in Upper School had. Each point represented a sum of money added to the basic annual salary, wherever you were on the incremental scale. Just over two years into the job I was still near the bottom, obviously.

I was thrilled, of course. Not only did I think it would be fun to run the library but I was delighted that Cedric – and he must have discussed it with people like Jack Rowlands before he made the offer – thought enough of me to promote me. Back home with Nick there were warm celebrations that evening, not to mention excited phone calls to my parents and anyone else I thought would be interested.

Then I had to decide how I was going to organise and run 'my' library to ensure that boys had as much access as possible while I continued with a full teaching timetable at the same time.

CHAPTER TEN

The library was basically a classroom in the heart of the building. At the top of the main central staircase on the first floor, it was to the right of the Head's office with the staffroom to the left and overlooking the playground as most rooms did. It was quite light and airy with a surprisingly good stock of fiction and non-fiction books.

During one English lesson a week most classes were brought into the library to look at, or borrow, books.

It seemed to me that I had two important jobs. One was to make the library as attractive and accessible as I could. The other was to find workable ways of keeping track of the stock for which I was now responsible. Not that anyone senior discussed such details with me or gave me any advice. Neither, of course, did I have any experience of running a library, anything remotely resembling a qualification in it, or a single hour of training. This was Creekside Comp after all. I was on my own and had to work out a *modus operandi* for myself.

Actually, if you're canny you can do well under a hands-off sink-or-swim style of management in a chaotic organisation. Anything that you do seems like an improvement and wins instant easy approval. It isn't difficult for the most ordinary of stars to twinkle brightly and be noticed, in a very dark sky.

Not that I'd quite worked that out as I embarked on librarianship. I was too busy trying to find ways of making it work and, with several classes, I still hadn't got the discipline right. There were third-year classes, in particular, that I found difficult to settle and I was still dealing with a lot of sexually-skewed insolence, especially from less able groups. Academically gifted they may not have been but they knew exactly how to make a young woman feel uncomfortable with their leers, asides and catcalls. And, even with a couple of years' survival to my credit, I certainly never arrived at school looking forward to a manageable straightforward day. Although most days had pleasant, satisfying bits – such as a first-year English class – there were still things to be dreaded every day.

And now there was the library. Since I had a full-time English timetable to teach as well, it was obvious I couldn't be in the library all the time. I wanted it to be open at breaks and lunchtimes too and I obviously couldn't manage that single-handedly either.

There was no question of leaving the library unlocked all day. Every Creekside Comp teacher walked about, jailer-like, with a large bunch of keys. No classroom or other teaching space was ever opened until the jailer – sorry, teacher – arrived to unlock it.

There were plenty of boys in Deptford who could get through any locked door in seconds. They'd been trained from infancy. I once saw this for myself when I lost the quite sturdy key to the cupboard in my classroom. Vexed because there were things in it I needed for the lesson, I said something which expressed irritation.

A boy in the front row got helpfully out of his place. 'Oh don't worry about that, Miss. I'll sort it. Got a hair pin?' I was so surprised that I pulled a pin out of my hair and gave it to him. In seconds he had picked the lock and my problem was solved. I thanked him profusely, of course, amazed at the casual way he admitted to this skill which, I'm sure, wasn't usually used to help teachers. I don't suppose he generally got thanked for it either.

As things were, the library would have to be locked unless a responsible person was present. Those were the rules.

So I needed help. And I knew where to find that. My original 1B boys were growing up fast but still around and as friendly and pleasant as ever. They also had the advantage, by then, of being lads I knew well enough to be able to trust completely.

Obviously they weren't all interested in helping Miss run her library. Many of them much preferred, and quite reasonably, to spend every spare minute playing football.

But a splendid little team of half a dozen apprentice librarians soon emerged, mostly from my first class but also from other classes I taught or had taught. They were, to a man, boys who needed a niche, liked books and were more comfortable with adults than the junior Deptford mafia or the football fanatics. They also knew each other very well. Quietish boys, on the whole, they had plenty to say for themselves in a context, which boosted their confidence. I guess they also liked being with me – partly as a mother or older sister figure but also, I'm sure, as a youngish woman they could fantasise about and swap thoughts with each other in private.

Mark Shaw, Percy Moulin, Paul Collier, Brian Penny and a lanky, earnest but bright boy called Owen Jones were the mainstay. And we were a team. They quickly mastered the procedures for checking books in and out and for shelving systematically. They were also good at coming up with ideas about how to do things better. I suppose today you'd call them 'proactive, empowered thinkers'.

And as for me, well it was, in effect, a management position in a very minor way. I had to manage both resources and people in order to provide a service to the community and to make things happen.

It felt very grown up – especially when I was assigned a pretty generous budget. Of course I knew that there were many different publishers – but had no real idea before becoming a school librarian, just how many. And this was long before most major book publishers merged and/or were taken over to form a small number of enormous companies with imprints, which is the situation today. I tried to assemble the current catalogues of as many publishers as I could. I kept them in a filing cabinet in alphabetical order by my desk in the library so I could refer to them when ordering.

I don't suppose there's a librarian in the country, in a school or anywhere else, who relies totally on paper catalogues today – although most publishers and imprints still produce them. But computers and online ordering were undreamt of in 1970.

What I did have to get to grips with pretty quickly were Standard Book Numbers or SBNs, very soon to develop into the ISBNs (International Standard Book Numbers), which are still with us. These were just getting established when I became a school librarian.

Individual schools didn't then manage their own budgets. All spending – apart from a tiny bit of petty cash – was done through the Local Education Authority: ILEA in our case. ILEA would assign to each school the spending of a block of money for resources and the Head, or someone senior, would divvy it out to the teachers in the schools who made the on-the-ground purchasing decisions – such as me and 'my' library.

But there was no scope for shopping about because everything had to come from County Hall or the suppliers with which it worked. When I ordered books I had to fill in an ILEA 'requisition' form, which would then be counter-signed by Cedric and despatched to County Hall.

A few weeks later, the books would arrive from County Hall, which had bought them on our behalf or supplied them from its own stock. It was cumbersome but probably didn't cost us any more than if we'd bought direct. Apart from a bit of publisher's discount for bulk purchase by education establishments, all books were then sold, under the net book agreement, at a price fixed by the publisher – an arrangement which finally collapsed in 1995.

My biggest fear in filling in those requisition forms was that I would make an error with those SBNs and end up with *Gray's Anatomy* instead of *Catcher in the Rye* or the *Kama Sutra* instead of *Boys' Own Book of Dinosaurs*. But it was probably a groundless fear because, very time-consumingly and tediously, you had to write the title as well.

So what sort of books did I buy? Lots of up-to-date fiction. It was at that time that I developed what was to become a lifelong habit of reading as much young adult and children's fiction as I can lay my hands on. Above all else I want young people to read lots of books. I was passionate about it then and still am. But you can encourage and promote reading only from a position of knowledge, strength and authority – and that means that successful teachers and librarians have to read a lot of books. Only then can you enthuse with all the passion that reading deserves.

Anything by Rosemary Sutcliff, Cynthia Harnett or Philippa Pearce seemed to go down well. So did the work of the wonderful Alan Garnett, especially *Elidor* (1965), which was fairly recent then. And I never met a Creekside Comp boy who wasn't transfixed by Reginald Maddox's *The Pit*, even if it had to be read aloud to him.

My young librarians started to read avidly too (an excellent side effect) and often made helpful suggestions about what we should order.

We didn't have to buy everything either. There was a magnificent library at County Hall – like a school library but much larger. I wonder what happened to it when ILEA disbanded and County Hall was sold to a Japanese developer who converted it into a tourist venue. Back in 1970 any school in the authority could augment its library stock by borrowing from County Hall for a block of time such as a term.

You could choose what you wanted by visiting or they would send a selection. I went there to choose several times. Rather like picking your goods in a modern supermarket and trolleying them up for later delivery you could go round the wonderful County Hall library and pull anything you fancied off the shelves. Then 'your' books were delivered in boxes by an ILEA van a week or two later. And it felt like Christmas in our library yet again.

On at least two occasions I took some of my library boys with me so that they could help choose. No rules to speak of then about pupils being driven in teachers' cars, although, through all the years I was a teacher, I paid for 'occasional professional use' insurance to cover that sort of situation.

I tried to keep the non-fiction stocks up to date and relevant too. That meant plenty of books about history, geography, science and so on. Other staff would sometimes send me lists of books relating to their subject which they thought should be in the library.

But I wanted the boys to come for pleasure as well as to find what they needed to know for homework, so I paid close attention to what they were interested in – football, obviously. That meant lots of books about the football celebrities of the day such as George Best and Jimmy Greaves.

Because the library was a much less formal environment than any classroom, being in it with boys was a good opportunity to chat open-endedly and find out what set them on fire. I was surprised to find that so many of them were 'into' tropical fish, for example, and made sure that our shelves had plenty of books about tetras, angel fish and so on and how to look after them. I got them at all reading levels from basic introductions meant for younger children through to quite adult reference books – so that any boy could read about his hobby whether he was a backward reader, an advanced one or something in between. Now they'd call it 'inclusivity'.

I also did a deal with the local newsagent – and Cedric organised a way of paying for it locally – so that we could have newspapers in the library every day during term time. We had two copies of the *Daily Express* and one of *The Times*. The newsagent put them aside for us and one of the ever-reliable library lads picked them up each morning and brought them into school.

And I didn't mind a bit if the boys merely turned to the backs of newspapers to read the sports pages. I just wanted to get them into the library and to develop the newspaper reading habit.

Also on our bill was *The Angling Times* – by far the most popular publication in the library. So popular that it was inclined to disappear and/or fall to pieces. I more or less solved that problem by buying three copies. It meant that they could almost always get access to it and nobody needed to nick it.

Sometimes, entirely spontaneously, they brought in things they wanted to talk about too. Colour supplements were beginning to appear with Sunday newspapers and they traded on very high standards of innovative photography.

I was quite moved when a third-year boy arrived in the library bearing one of these. His eyes were shining with excitement. 'Just look, Miss,' he said, completely without embarrassment, forgetting briefly perhaps that I wasn't an older sister. 'Have you seen these?' He wanted me to share with him the marvel of the first colour photographs of babies in the womb which any of us had ever seen.

Some lads would have giggled. This one just wanted to communicate how deeply stirred he was by both the subject matter and the photography. It was one of those moments all teachers treasure – when you remember just why you went into the profession. I just loved the idea of his gathering up the magazine at home and saying or thinking, 'I must take this to school to show Mrs Elkin in case she hasn't seen them and to find out what she thinks.'

While I was immersed in the joys of librarianship, just outside the library door, Cedric was busy reforming the school.

Goodness knows how he screwed so much money out of ILEA but within weeks of arrival he seemed to be making new appointments every day.

We were destined to be one school based mostly on the Creekside site, so suddenly we were knee-deep in heads of department. Not the absentee other-end-of-Deptford type we'd been used to but dynamic, keen types who were with us every day trying to manage us.

Peter Beach became Cedric's new deputy, which meant the appointment of a new Head of English – Fred Tomlinson. Actually many of Cedric's appointments were pretty good but he must have been having an off day when he took on namby pamby, ineffectual, inefficient Fred. Yes, he was there and he was pleasant enough but absent when dynamism was given out, so it was a missed opportunity.

We also got a new Head of Maths, a large self-important man who once told me that I obviously never did any housework because my nails were too long. Where was Germaine Greer when I needed her? Des Wood was quite well known locally because he was also on Lewisham Borough Council (for the Labour Party) and annoyed a lot of people there too.

Derek Cathcart, the new Head of Science, was a gruff, burly man in his late forties. Like most of his contemporaries his young manhood had been dominated by war. And Derek had quite a story to tell, although it was, inevitably, Geoff who coaxed it out of him, not me.

According to Geoff, Derek had been taken prisoner of war and incarcerated somewhere in Central Europe. He and another man somehow managed to escape and set out to walk to freedom. Dodging the many and various dangers they encountered on the way, and eating and sleeping when and where they could, they spent many months walking to neutral Sweden. There they made their way to a port where a ship bound for Britain was being loaded with timber. How to get aboard as stowaways? On the dockside they simply picked up a plank, one at each end and marched casually and confidently up the gangway with it. A few days later Derek was back in Blighty.

Teaching science must have seemed tame by comparison but Derek was effective in the classroom and made sure the department was led rather than simply allowed to drift as before.

At about the same time, new Heads of History, Geography and RE also appeared.

Cedric also went for Year Heads in a big way. Suddenly we had highly paid staff, mostly new external appointments, teaching light timetables. Their main job was to work with form tutors across year groups but nothing they did seemed to make much difference and I suspect for most it was a pretty cushy number. They all had cosy offices to hide in – to Geoff's fury because he didn't really rate any job in a school apart from being in a classroom with kids.

Peter Beach never seemed to do much Deputy Heading in any meaningful way either. Mostly he walked two paces behind Cedric as the latter strutted regally round the corridors. If it was a royal procession Peter was the attendant. He always looked worried and ill-at-ease. Cedric believed that we should all work together to deal with, for instance, the school's appalling litter problem and often lectured the staff about it.

If Cedric saw a piece of litter on one of his corridor processions he would point and say loudly, 'Litter, Mr Beach, litter!' and Peter would pick it up.

Submissive, self-effacing bag carrying didn't seem to do Peter any long-term damage though. A few years after Cedric's arrival, Peter left the school for a headship of his own. 'And it's such a huge place that his salary starts where Cedric's leaves off,' Geoff informed me.

Cedric also seemed to believe that a mixed staff would civilise a boys' school. Heloise hadn't returned after her maternity leave and for a while I'd again been the only woman on the teaching staff. But not for much longer.

His first female appointment was Lyn Tindell. Her job was to teach drama. Yes, drama. The idea of treating drama as a separate *bona fide* subject was pretty progressive for Creekside Comp.

Before Lyn's arrival there was a vague expectation that English teachers might do some drama and there'd been a production or two. Pat McGuire, during an unusual sober period when he actually came to school, had directed some sixth-form boys from 'the other end' in a decentish production of Robert Bolt's play

Beckett, inadequately staged in our hall in Lower School. But in general, drama had been conspicuously absent at Creekside Comp unless you count the unintentional sort of which there was plenty.

Lyn was in her mid-twenties. She was tall, slim and pretty in a Diana, Princess of Wales kind of way, except that she was dark-haired. This being the early '70s she wore very short skirts, half the length of mine, above her fetching long legs, and some of her tops were lowish in cut. She also wore masses of the inky smudgy eye makeup which was fashionable at the time.

She had some good ideas and was a dedicated teacher but she was too much, far too much, for the rampant adolescents of Creekside Comp. It must be very hard when being good looking and attractive goes against you. But partly, perhaps, because she was teaching an informal touchy-feely subject she was the victim of what would now be called sexual harassment from day one.

As Geoff said, she hadn't got the measure of just how testosterone-fuelled fourteen-year-old boys in Deptford functioned. She didn't seem remotely like a mum, or even an older sister. Her appearance shouted at Deptford youth the only other sort of woman they knew. 'I'm afraid they just see the way she dresses as an invitation,' said Geoff.

She frequently had problems in class when boys would sidle up to her and try to get a hand up her skirt. In all the five years I was there, serious as some of my problems were, I managed to avoid that. I suppose she tried to deal with it with gentleness and jokes, which would have reinforced the mixed message. Soon she was complaining to Cedric – which must have taken courage. He would then berate the offending classes or boys, which probably made things worse.

Then disaster struck. Or almost. Lyn was set upon by a group of four Creekside Comp boys as she walked on her own through St Paul's churchyard. I don't think it was a full rape but it came close and was nasty. She, obviously, knew who the assailants were and, highly distressed, reported them by name to Cedric.

He should, without doubt, have involved the police, but he didn't. Sexual assault is after all a very serious offence. I suppose he didn't want to engender negative publicity for the school. What Cedric actually did was most unwise. He called a full assembly and lined the culprits up on the stage. He then told the whole school what had happened and made those four shifty boys listen while he told the 'audience' what they'd done, forcefully expressing his utter horror and disgust.

I have rarely seen adolescents look so uncomfortable as those four boys. And because of that there was a wave of something approaching sympathy from the lads listening in the hall. Cedric was in serious danger of making heroes of the boys he wanted so much to punish.

If Cedric had lived in the eighteenth century or earlier, I expect he would have been a devotee of the stocks, the pillory or even slicing off ears and the like. It was an attitude which sat oddly with his Labour Party politics. There was nothing liberal about the left as far as Cedric was concerned.

But he worried about Lyn and I suspect the implications of having women on the staff were giving him sleepless nights. Perhaps it was Mrs Flyte, wanting a bit of peace at home, who suggested the revolutionary Trousers Policy.

In the early 1970s, trousers were not generally regarded as smart dress for women. There'd been well-publicised cases of women being denied access to formal dress events because they were wearing trouser suits. Even seven years later when I started in a girls' secondary school in Kent, the prissy female Head was adamant that she would not have her teachers wearing 'slacks' to work.

But Cedric evidently decided that he'd rest easier at night if the legs (and a few other things) of his female staff were safely encased in trousers, although at the same time he was trying to impose ties on the men, some of whom were reluctant. Considering what an in-your-face type he usually was, Cedric's trouser campaign was almost subtle. He let it casually be known via Peter Beach and Jack Rowlands that trousers might, just might, be a good idea and oh, so smart and warm and comfortable. Jack Rowlands could hardly keep a straight face when he shared this with me.

On one occasion I was standing in the bottom corridor reading something on a noticeboard. I was wearing a pair of navy blue crimplene flares (well, it *was* 1971) with a long paisley blouse – the sort of outfit which would have been frowned upon by most secondary school heads at the time. Cedric walked past.

'Oh, Susan, don't you look nice?' he said in a warm, sugary voice. 'I think that's an ideal way to dress for school. So sensible.' I don't think he was carrying a palette knife but he certainly laid it on thick.

The new policy must have been quite a disappointment for Mike Churchill who was still very much around, teaching plumbing and salivating over legs protruding, by then, from various people's mini-skirts.

Other young women started to appear in the staffroom too, including a large new graduate whose father was a coal miner in Nottingham and a sparkling black woman who – rather disconcertingly because it was something I knew about only from newspapers – was an active member of the militant group Black Power. Then there was another young English teacher who soon married someone she met at Creekside Comp and went on, eventually, to be Head of a major London girls' school.

Soon, as part of the many changes going on in the building, we were assigned a proper, decent ladies' loo. It was actually the one used by the men at the top of the stairs when I first went to the school. It was all done up and the urinals, I suppose, removed because there was no sign of them when I began using the facility. The men were, from then on, accommodated elsewhere in the building.

CHAPTER ELEVEN

Cedric was single-mindedly determined to reinvent Creekside Comp as a single school on one site. Of course that wasn't logistically quite possible but his policy was clearly to make 'our' building the heart of the school and rename the other, former Upper School, 'the annexe'.

So suddenly we had boys of all ages having lessons in the Creek Road building. I saw sixth formers – a rather select group because most boys still left at fifteen or sixteen – around the corridors every day. And suddenly I seemed to be in the thick of O Level, CSE and those euphemistically named 'non-exam' – that is weak ability – classes determined to leave school as soon as they could. But I still wasn't teaching any senior classes myself.

Some classes continued to be taught nearly a mile away in the other building and until Cedric worked out a way of streamlining it there was a fair amount of cross-Deptford movement. The staff drove, of course, and gave lifts to non-car-owning colleagues. Boys were meant to walk. Depleted classes were inevitable. Many boys, less than keen on school, education and teachers, lost themselves during the walk and failed to appear at the destination. They must have thought Cedric's new pan-Deptford policy was a real gift.

I was never involved in these migrations and continued to be based – part of a much larger staff than before – in Creek Road.

Ted Hill, who taught English, was one of the many staff who'd long worked in the other building but whom I didn't really know until Cedric moved most teachers to Creek Road.

I think there'd once been a Mrs Hill but she'd long since seen sense and left. Ted was fussy and querulous in an old maidish way. Geoff had known him for years and found him tiresome and sometimes eccentric – the latter a bit rich coming from Geoff.

Ted's USP within the school was that he was keen on choral speaking and ran a choral speaking 'choir' which spoke poems in chorus, really quite well. Incongruous as it was for that setting, it probably exposed the boys involved to poetry they wouldn't otherwise have encountered and must have improved their oral and projection skills.

Otherwise Ted sat lugubriously in the staffroom and told us unlikely things in a humourless way. Clearly a lonely insomniac, he thought nothing of driving, say, to Eastbourne and back during the night just for something to do. The mileage on his newish car was extraordinarily high, so what he said was evidently true.

Then he told us that he thought he'd like a dog to take for walks and for company. So he went to Battersea Dogs' Home – now Battersea Dogs and Cats Home – and arranged to adopt a magnificent Dalmatian. It was not a happy marriage.

As Geoff observed with his trademark barbed accuracy, no one gives away a 'magnificent Dalmatian' which would have cost its original owner a fortune unless there was something seriously wrong with it. Ted's dog was, quite literally, barking mad. When it wasn't – well – barking, it seized every opportunity to escape from the hand which fed it. On one occasion it charged off into the streets of Forest Hill and Sydenham – Ted lived on the SE23/ SE26 border – with Ted chasing impotently behind it for hours.

He kept the animal less than a week before returning the poor, traumatised (I presume) beast to Battersea.

Not long after that he moved out to a village named Pratt's Bottom near Bromley. At that time there was a waist-high road sign declaring the village's rather odd, arguably ambiguous, name on a sign on the A21 just outside Ted's house. He never tired of telling us in self-righteous, droning, but prurient tones about all the people who photographed each other in obscene poses by the sign. In the end the council must have got fed up with complaints too because the only sign on that spot now is ten feet high beside the dual carriageway.

But in school the highlight of Ted's week was the arrival of the *Amateur Photographer* magazine, one of the publications bought by the school for the staffroom entertainment, along with the *Times Educational Supplement, The Guardian* and one or two other things. I'm not sure how interested Ted actually was in photography, but the magazine always included some 'life studies' – i.e. female nudes – and those were what Ted invariably turned to first, trying desperately to look casual but always failing.

I met Mr Kenilworth too. Another one-off. He was an overweight, gravel-voiced, bearded man of indeterminate age, most of whose breakfast – yesterday's and the day before's as well as today's – was usually smeared down his tie. Physically unprepossessing as he was, 'Kenny', yet another man who seemed never to have been graced with a given name, was so knowledgeable that it was, quite literally, awe inspiring.

Kenny's hobby was getting degrees – masters and doctorates mostly. He had originally read law at university and may, at some stage about a century before I met him, have practised law. It was still the law which fascinated him, although he was no mean historian. Every two or three years he completed his current degree, his subjects becoming progressively more obscure. Then he would simply start another. He wasn't interested in pieces of paper or post-nominal letters. He just liked structured learning. Other men collect stamps or play badminton. Kenny did degrees.

Coral Miles, Geoff's wife, who worked with research scientists, couldn't imagine how Kenny was still managing to find people to supervise his doctorates in the abstruse areas in which he, Kenny, was the acknowledged expert. She thought he was, effectively, self-supervised – a one-man higher-degree generator, as it were.

So Kenny was quite an institution but worked only with the older boys, which was why my path and his didn't cross until the arrival of Cedric the Unifier. He didn't do anything as menial as look after a tutor group and most of the time he was in the staffroom so his timetable must have been very light.

I was once present during one of his lessons because for some reason he had nowhere to take his class and I offered him the library as long as he didn't mind me pottering in the background.

His class consisted of four or five well-behaved young men taking A Level law. They sat in a semi-circle while Kenny, noteless of course, poured information at them in his own monotonous way. It was hardly inspired teaching but the lads seemed to be engaged. One or two of them even asked questions occasionally. As I listened I rejoiced that I'd never been taught by anyone like Kenny. Of course he knew his stuff but he neither knew nor cared how to be dynamic. I'd have been asleep in minutes.

Amazingly there was a Mrs Kenilworth, who clearly had no truck with taking her husband's ties to the dry cleaner. His daughter, aged about twenty, was at university. After listening to him talking at length in the staffroom about his Anne, the darling of his life, the penny dropped: Anne Kenilworth. She'd been at grammar school with me, two or three years behind me. But I knew her name because she'd been a super-bright high achiever whose name was often read out in assembly for coming top, winning prizes and so on.

Hard to reconcile this very bright young thing with seedy Kenny. 'Actually impossible to imagine Kenny being active enough to engender a child even twenty years ago,' said the acid Geoff, who thought about sex about as often as men are apocryphally supposed to.

Also now based in our building was the Headmaster's secretary, Mrs Edith Bridges. She'd been on the staff for some time and had worked for Harry Baker but, naturally, she'd been closeted away in the other building, and I didn't meet her until Cedric came.

She was every inch an old-fashioned, very able and efficient administrator. Tall, discreetly dressed in mid-calf straight skirts, she was around fifty when she was moved to Creek Road.

Cedric had installed himself in the large first-floor office previously used by Jack Rowlands or Jim O'Riordan. Jack was rehoused in a smaller office along the corridor and Jim finally disappeared within weeks of Cedric's arrival. When I last heard of Jim he was teaching junior maths, without any extra responsibilities, at the school in Peckham where his wife taught, and seemed to be holding things together – a classic case of a man promoted beyond his competence, I suppose.

Cedric placed Edith in the room immediately below his so that her office near the main door became what we would now call 'Reception'. Janet and Margaret assisted her there. And another woman worked part-time in the other building.

She was astonishingly sharp. One day Edith asked me, on behalf of Cedric, whether I would like to go to a performance of *The Gondoliers* at a school in Woolwich. Cedric had been invited but couldn't go. Would I like to represent him? 'I know you like Gilbert and Sullivan so I suggested you to the Headmaster,' said Edith, usually addressed as Mrs Bridges, to whom, at that stage I had hardly spoken.

'How on earth did you know that?' I asked her, astonished. 'Oh just something you said one day about, "like Pooh Bah, not even being there",' she answered. Clearly a woman who docketed things away, she'd have made a good police officer. She certainly made sure that, administratively, the school ran as smoothly as it possibly could.

Edith's new office, to the fury of many of the old guard, was the former staff dining room. It was the room where staff who weren't on duty had been used to eating lunch in peace rather than in Andy Andrews' 'piggery'. But Cedric would have none of it.

He believed – and he was probably right – that if most staff ate in the same room as the pupils the very presence of adults would have a beneficial effect on behaviour.

So now there were rows of tables reserved for staff in one corner of the canteen. We got our food from a different 'express' hatch but it was the same food and it wasn't bad. There was a new cook who was Italian, another of Cedric's appointments, and some pretty decent stuff came out of the kitchen considering this was 'school dinners' – including good salads which I was more than happy to eat.

Cedric did several things to embed this policy. Hitherto staff had paid for any school meal eaten on days when they weren't on duty. Anyone on duty got a free meal. Cedric now said that any member of staff who ate in the canteen with the boys, was effectively doing a duty – helping to supervise merely by being present. That meant, he said, that anyone eating in the canteen need not pay for his or her meal. Over the course of a term it added up to quite a saving and it certainly stopped too many people from reacting to the new policy by bolting to the staffroom with sandwiches brought from home.

He was also scrupulous about being seen eating in the canteen himself and took all his important visitors there too, so that they could meet staff informally and so that the boys could see it happening.

Cedric's real *tour de force* came at Christmas. We would send the boys home early and have a staff Christmas dinner later upstairs, he said. But first he wanted every member of staff in the canteen serving the boys, so that for once the kids got special occasion table service with waiters rather than having to line up and jostle cafeteria style.

So we did. Or at least most of us did. And it worked beautifully. The climax was the entrance of Cedric himself, clad in a chef's tall white hat bearing a gigantic Christmas pudding. All credit to him. It was a lovely idea. Many of our boys would have come from families for whom pleasant Christmas traditions were thin on the ground and this gave them something good to look back on and remember with affection.

No head I worked for after Cedric – and there were to be eight more in various schools – ever did what he did, or anything remotely like it, to give the kids a treat at Christmas. Hair was let down but it was, of course, actually an inspired way of establishing discipline – and so different from his usual style.

And Cedric's 'usual style' included the issue of Ellis's Finger. Ellis was a hard-to-handle lad in the fourth year. Like the rest of his year he now came regularly to Creek Road for woodwork lessons. Woodwork was big in the school and of course the ever-reliable Ray Weston could not teach every lesson himself. One of his assistants was a basically decent, but utterly ineffectual little man named Al Coster. Al had done something else for some years (worked as a chippy?) and come into teaching as a less than bright mature entrant to the profession.

He was earnest and boring. He was also dangerously incompetent. An incident in the woodwork shop with Ellis's class – presumably fooling about and inadequately supervised – led to a dreadful accident with a band saw. Horrifyingly, the index finger on Ellis's left hand was severed.

As far as I know, the boy's parents, in that pre-litiginous age, accepted it as an accident and didn't sue. But within school there was a big question mark over what Cedric would do about Al Coster, who evidently should not be in a woodwork shop in charge of boys.

Instead of opening disciplinary proceedings leading to dismissal, which is what Cedric should have done, he asked his minions how old Al was and offered him early retirement.

'Right, come on, girl, let's go and chop a few fingers off,' said Geoff, managing his fury by disguising it as humorous bitterness as usual. 'Then we can all go years before our time on full pension.' Cedric certainly didn't always get things right.

His installation of a 'management team' was probably a bit hasty and tactless, for example. The school had always had a culture of everyone – except maybe Harry Baker – mucking in and doing a fair bit of teaching. Yes, we had a lot of absenteeism and far more than our fair share of other problems but hitherto everyone who was actually there saw classroom work as the core of the school's activity.

How old-fashioned. Suddenly we had Cedric. Peter Beach was appointed his deputy and neither man ever sullied his hands with a lesson. Teaching, it seemed, was clearly beneath them.

To make matters worse there were three others with titles such as Director of Studies, Head of Pastoral Care and Head of Upper School. Each had an office, strode around the building clutching sheaves of paper and attended a lot of mysterious meetings. Some were new appointments from outside. Others were sudden elevations for old stagers.

What they all had in common was that each was highly paid and none did any teaching – pretty hard to stomach such generals given the hours of cover we poor bloody infantrymen were still doing every week. It was the sort of policy which makes teachers justifiably cross. Of course a school has to be managed and we sorely needed some better management but this was overkill, to put it mildly. Geoff dubbed the management quintet 'the furtive five' and that was one of the politer names they were given.

Meanwhile strange things, which didn't have a lot to do with teaching English or running a library, were wont to happen in my classroom. The things had fur coats, four legs and a tail.

Next to the school, behind the huts which housed most of the craft workshops, was a triangular patch of wasteland. It was probably half an acre or more and may have been a bomb site, or part of one.

In the late 1960s and early '70s it was overgrown with weeds and bushes and strewn with much unappealing rubbish – the odd old fridge or mattress – dumped there by untidy locals. So there was plenty of cover for wildlife. The urban fox was a creature of the future. Back then the colonisers were feral felines which bred prolifically as cats left to their own fecund devices will.

Nested wherever female cats could find cover there were, therefore, a lot of kittens – scrawny, flea bitten and many probably diseased. Sometimes a kitten would be abandoned, its mother lost (killed on the road or savaged by a dog?) or somehow separated from its litter.

The younger boys who knew me well were more than aware of my penchant for cats. Although I never encouraged it, if they spotted a kitten, as they saw it, in need they were inclined to gather it up and bring it in to me. 'Let's take it to Miss. She'll know what to do.'

I found myself having to make arrangements for hapless kittens on several occasions. The worst was when some of our elder boys had gone on to the wasteland, found a lost kitten, picked it up and started throwing it from one to the other like a ball for sport. 'My' boys were outraged. I never found out how they got the poor beast away from its tormentors in one piece but somehow they did and there it was in my classroom in desperate need of a bit of love.

On every occasion I managed to find a boy somewhere in the school who said his family would give the kitten a home. Each time I spoke to the parents and it seemed initially to be OK.

But at least once, inevitably, it wasn't OK at all. These animals were semi-wild. Perhaps their ancestors had once been fireside cats – although in Deptford it's more likely they lived a rough life as ratters – but these descendants had no refined manners. The kittens were sweet but, like tiger cubs, they soon began to display the wild scratching and biting habits of wild cats which made them almost impossible to domesticate.

So, all in all, my well-intended efforts as a one-woman cat charity were not particularly successful. One mother wrote to me very cross that I had foisted a wild cat on her rather than some placid moggy. Well, she knew where it had come from. What on earth did she expect?

CHAPTER TWELVE

As well as imposing a management team, Cedric was adamant that part of the school's problem was a high number of 'remedial' – the 1970s term for special needs – pupils whose needs were not only unmet but largely ignored.

So Cedric appointed two women to sort it out. They were Bess Yates – who some years later would marry Jack Rowlands for a while when he tired of his then wife – and Celia Smith.

Bess was a special needs expert in her thirties and Celia younger. I don't think they knew each other before but they'd been appointed to work together and were a well-bonded team from day one. Their brief – or what they took as their brief – was to raise the boys' reading levels.

She was really the first specialist in this field I ever met. Special needs were almost unmentioned at college and no one had paid any attention to them for the first three years I was at Creekside Comp. I disliked what she did but would have been hard put to explain why at the time. Working with SEN teachers, of varying approach and effectiveness, for many years afterwards showed me what Bess's problem was.

She had a Method. And she imposed it like a blanket on every boy in the class. There was no sense that what works for one pupil might not work for another and that to meet needs you have to treat people as individuals. Personalised learning and theories about different learning styles hadn't been invented but I sensed that somehow this wasn't the best way of helping struggling readers.

Bess's method was big boxes of very expensive colour-coded, graded comprehension work cards. The idea was that each boy was tested for reading level and then assigned to the right colour level. He had to read the card and then answer multiple-choice questions designed to show that the reading really had been understood and internalised. Success at several of these would lead to promotion to the next colour level and Progress You Can Measure.

In the early seventies, I knew little about Einstein and his pertinent comments on almost everything. 'What counts cannot be counted' was surely one of his best aphorisms and Bess's remedial reading system could have been invented to illustrate it.

Another problem with it was that the system was American, so that the cards were rather unhelpfully written in US English with American cultural assumptions. They were also desperately boring and samey – nothing remotely literary or imaginative. Today I'd deem them deeply patronising. It seemed to me that such formulaic work would simply put the boys off reading. And I must have been right because I haven't heard of any school using this sort of scheme for a long time.

The reason I knew about it in such detail was that Bess and Celia worked in a room to which those of us with classes categorised as in need of remedial reading were timetabled to take our classes for one or two lessons a week. It meant that for those sessions the boys had three 'cruising' teachers in the room, which should have been a real bonus. Somehow I always felt we were all expending a great deal of energy but missing something crucial and failing many of the boys we were trying to teach.

Not that the boys complained. Many of the underachievers were biddable, quiet, rather sad individuals well used to slipping through the net. At least in Bess's sessions they were getting a loud, clear message that someone cared and was prepared to help – even if, in my view, the nature of the help was seriously misguided. Frankly it never seemed like 'proper' teaching to me and I used to find the sessions led by Bess very boring.

I never actually saw the old Upper School library which Ted Hill had run. Once he arrived in our building he ceased to have any responsibility for it.

One day Cedric sent for me. He wanted to talk about merging the books repository, which was still languishing in the annexe, and 'my' friendly little library next to his office.

Now that so many older boys were having most of their lessons in Creek Road, they needed access to books with age- and subject-relevant books.

What Cedric proposed was to have all the books – and some of the shelves to put them on – transported to me. I would then, somehow, have to find a way of accommodating them in the same space.

Of course he 'couldn't' offer me any more money for doubling the size of my job at a stroke – he was a head after all and I wasn't a member of the furtive five, nor likely to be at age twenty-three – but he did have a bargaining tool or two up his sleeve.

He would give me all the annual budget Ted Hill had had to spend on new books plus a bit more. It could be added to the pretty generous budget I already had.

Now books money is music to the ears of any bookish person or librarian and the £2,000 on the table was a fabulous sum for the time. My salary was by then about £1,100. The proposed new library budget was almost double that – say around £55,000 in today's money. You can buy a lot of books for that.

The second 'sweetener' was the promise of two more 'free' periods a week so that I'd have more time for the library. I suppose he meant well. Perhaps he'd forgotten that teachers at my level spent most of their non-teaching time covering for absent colleagues. Members of the furtive five just doled out cover to other people. They did none themselves.

So the latter wasn't much of an incentive. Nonetheless I agreed to do it, reasoning (with a bit of counselling from my father) that

I needed as much experience as I could get and this new challenge could be quite fun.

A week or two later the books arrived – tea chest after tea chest of them. It felt like having someone move into your home with all their possessions, while everything you own is still in situ. And it certainly meant that 'my' tidy library suddenly looked as if a hurricane had hit it and it was very hard indeed for boys of any age to access.

So the need for some rigorous sorting was urgent. The former Lower School library had shelves lining the three sides which weren't windows. Now, at Cedric's suggestion, we put the 'new' double-sided bookcases in at right-angles with about five feet between them. It created alcoves and gave us twice or three times as much shelving space. It meant, however, that there was no longer enough space for tables and desks to accommodate a class of thirty, so the library would have to be used differently in future.

I began to unpack the boxes and tea chests. There were lots of treasures therein – such as a complete *Oxford English Dictionary*. No twenty-first-century secondary school would dream of such a purchase. For years it would have been far too expensive. Now you'd simply have it online.

So there was quite a frisson in opening each crate to find out what it held. It was also a dauntingly big job. Geoff and Jack Rowlands suggested that they come in for a day with me at half term and that the three of us would have an uninterrupted bash at getting those books onto shelves in some sort of order.

To be honest it was not entirely satisfactory because there simply wasn't time to re-catalogue every book, which was the only way I would ever have been able to absorb the newly arrived books and keep proper tabs on them. But I did my best. And the boy librarians, some of whom came in to help on the same half-term day as Geoff and Jack, worked very hard at it too. Mark Shaw, for example, was delighted to be part of the project and happily agreed to come into school to do a grown-up job. I picked him up from the end of his road and dropped him back there at the end of the day.

I had tremendous fun extending the library still further with thousands of new books too – given the lovely budget I'd got.

What I didn't realise was that Cedric, who was quite prescient and forward-looking, knew that things would move on and that this quart-into-a-pint-pot library arrangement would be pretty temporary.

Perhaps he also knew before I did that my circumstances and role in the school would soon change drastically.

In the early summer of 1971, I discovered I was pregnant – not that it was a surprising discovery. Nick and I had been married for two years and were both keen, products of our generation, to get a family underway while we were still young. Starting a baby was, thank goodness, no problem at all and we virtually planned the birth date.

I confided in Geoff – I think he'd sensed it long before I told him – and then went to see Cedric.

'I've come to resign,' I said. 'I'm having a baby in January so I have to give you notice.'

'Oh no, you don't want to resign,' he said, pulling his NUT diary out of his pocket to consult the information therein. 'There's a new system now for women having babies. You get paid leave and then some more money when you return.'

'But I'm not planning to come back (famous last words!),' I replied. 'I'm going to stay at home and look after my child.'

'Doesn't matter,' said Cedric. 'Anyone having a baby, regardless of what they plan to do afterwards, is entitled to this new maternity leave. And anyway, I hope I shall be able to persuade you not to leave us altogether. I'm sure we can arrange for you to do a bit of part-time and you could bring the baby with you.'

Perhaps he wasn't such a bad head after all. And I was certainly very touched by how much he seemed to want me on his staff.

And yes, maternity leave was a very new idea. Until that moment I had never heard of it and knew no one who'd benefited from it. Four years later – when I was in another school in another part of the country – and pregnant with my second child, I had to tell the incredulous Head and his secretary that I wanted maternity leave while they stared at me in disbelief.

It was a pretty good deal too. Schools were obsessed with not having women in late pregnancy on site, so your leave compulsorily began eleven weeks before the due date. You got several months on full pay and then several more on half salary, with some of it backdated when you returned to work. It certainly eased things for a young couple who expected, and had planned, to live for a while on one income instead of two.

But none of it was going to happen for several months. Back at school I had to teach the rest of the summer term and – it worked out quite neatly – until the autumn half term. I had a bit of nausea in the early weeks, sore nipples and was given to fits of feeling very cold but otherwise I felt fine and it was business as usual.

Cedric had, perforce, appointed a music teacher to replace Timmy Fletcher. And the new music man couldn't have been more different. Olaf Andersen was a tall, good-looking, very charismatic black man in his late forties. For months he sat in the staffroom staring inscrutably into the distance without speaking to anyone. But gradually he unwound and became quite a force for good in the school.

Although he was a likeable and attractive character, his background was as mysterious as Pete Sargeant's. And like Pete's his stories tended to change so, to this day, I don't really know what his background was. The account we got most often was that his black Dutch mother had been a servant in the Dutch Embassy in one of the Central American countries. He claimed to be her illegitimate child, fathered by the ambassador, which would have made him mixed race.

Well, he certainly had the sort of elegance and bearing you might expect in the well-educated son of a diplomat, so perhaps his father had paid for his schooling. Olaf's own children – a son and a daughter – were clearly both comfortably off with good jobs. His wife, he said, had died.

He was a fine musician – a concert-standard pianist and no mean violinist. When he finally moved on he went to America to tour the 'hick' towns playing concertos with local orchestras. He wasn't an A team professional musician but clearly well able to earn a living by performing. It was always a mystery to me – and he never told us what had happened – how he came to be on the staff at Creekside Comp. It wasn't, by and large, a school people queued up to work in, even under Cedric, and a man with Olaf's talents could probably, if everything were as it seemed, have got a job anywhere.

His presence meant that music began to permeate the school. He got some of the boys singing in choirs and playing instruments. Several of us on the staff could play instruments and we used to go along to Olaf's classroom at lunchtime and after school to practise as a group. I had played violin at school from age seven and still played in a local orchestra, Geoff – with his usual quirky approach to things – had taught himself the flute, Jack Rowlands was quite competent on clarinet and there were one or two others.

Olaf would arrange pieces for the group. We played, for example, part of one of the Mozart piano concertos. He played the piano part and arranged the orchestral parts for his motley little band. He and I would amuse ourselves with Bach's pieces for two violins too. It was a pleasant oasis in the middle of the school day and somehow at odds with the culture of the school – cor blimey Deptford raging around us as we bashed out a bit of Beethoven.

Inevitably, boys got wind of what we were doing and, in some cases, role modelling worked its magic. Olaf was able to arrange lessons for interested boys and even asked me to do beginner violin lessons with one lad, which I did for a term or two.

At the end of the summer term Cedric decided that we'd have a proper Speech Day in the main hall at nearby Goldsmiths College, then mostly a teacher training establishment, now part of the University of London. Nothing like this had been attempted at Creekside Comp in living memory. Olaf – and those of us who were wont to support him – was asked to provide lots of music because, typically for a head, Cedric was determined that his Speech Day should be a showcase for achievement. And all heads morph into music lovers for Speech Day or prizegiving – even if they can't tell Elgar from the Beatles for the other 364 days in the year.

We managed to field quite an orchestra. Among other things we performed 'Sunrise Sunset' from *Fiddler on the Roof*, which Olaf, as usual, arranged for the forces at his disposal. He wrote very easy parts for beginner instrumentalists, got those of us who could to do the more elaborate bits and incorporated some fancy stuff for a boy of Afro-Caribbean background who'd discovered a talent for percussion. 'It's in the blood with some of them – goes back to jungle drums,' said Geoff, as usual putting his finger on the truth, even if it was arguably racist. Olaf conducted.

And when we sang 'Jerusalem' (no half measures for Cedric) Olaf could, unsurprisingly, play that challenging introduction which frightens off many quite competent pianists. 'I think I'm the only person present who can sing "Jerusalem" without the bloody words,' said Geoff, conscientiously doing just that. 'It takes an atheist.'

For this event Cedric wheeled in several dignitaries for gravitas – cronies of his from the Department of Education and Science and the Inner London Education Authority – and someone from the Borough of Lewisham who spoke both badly and at length.

And when I wasn't playing the violin, trying to drum some English into boys whose levels of receptiveness were variable and reorganising my mini empire in the library, I was getting more and more pregnant.

It could have been a giggling-have-you-had-sex-Miss?' matter with the less mature of my students. I dealt with it by being blunt, matter-of-fact and pretending, at least, to be totally unembarrassed. 'I'm having a baby in January,' I told my classes firmly – daring them to snigger. 'That means I shall be leaving in November and another teacher will take you for English.'

I developed, and later almost made a speciality of, that matter-of-fact technique. I quickly learned that if you need (or want) to discuss sex, bodily functions or anything potentially delicate in class, it is usually easy to get round the potential problems. You simply say what you mean calmly using proper adult words – and don't bat an eyelid or allow a shred of awkwardness to show.

Many years later as Head of Upper School in a girls' comprehensive I had to do the sex education classes for a frumpy spinster of a form teacher who went green at the very idea. I could look the girls straight in the eye and say 'erect penis' as easily as I might have said 'exercise book' while colleagues agonised in the staffroom about this challenging task they had to face. Creekside Comp was a good training ground in more than one way.

In the same way I gradually worked out a few ways of averting avoidable classroom chaos. When it was a case of *sauve qui peut*, this 1960s girl was damn well going to swim not sink.

One of my most difficult classes was inclined to swarm into the room as the boys arrived at the door – in twos and threes, although they were supposed to line up outside the door and file in when invited. In practice, when the likes of 3F turned up they would saunter in when they felt like it. I might start a conversation with the early arrivals only to have it completely (and deliberately) disrupted by a couple more who would, from the doorway, start shouting something, usually mildly offensive, at their mates across the room.

'Apple crumble makes you grumble, apple tart makes you fart' was a favourite. So was drawing a cartoon of a penis if they could grab a pen or piece of chalk – just a single line forming a long inverted 'u' shape with a dot near the end. This was universally known as a 'helmet' and was meant to make me feel uncomfortable – which it did, of course, not because it was a penis but because it was a sign I was losing, or had never had, control.

An even worse mistake, I discovered, was to delay starting the lesson, such as it was, because I knew half the class wasn't there – probably pissing up the walls in the lavatories as a way of delaying arrival in my classroom.

And worse still was trying to make an entrance yourself when the class, or most of it, was already assembled, tempting as it often was to put off confronting them as long as possible. 'Always get there before the little buggers. It gives you the upper hand,' opined Geoff.

So that's what I tried to do – and it stood me in good stead for the rest of my thirty-six-year teaching career. When I was expecting a difficult class at Creekside Comp I would have the work I wanted them to do written on the board before they arrived. Then I would stand by the door with a pile of marked exercise books. As each boy walked in I would say, 'Here's your book. Work's on the board. Sit down and start straightaway, please.' It certainly helped and just occasionally we had something approaching an orderly lesson.

And although the 'difficult' type of boy with an image to maintain and dominated by peer pressure would never have admitted it, most quite liked the idea that you'd actually marked their books – there was an awful lot of unmarked work at Creekside Comp given the patchy competence of so many of the staff. Boys might have been forgiven for thinking that nobody cared what they did or whether they did any work or made any progress.

Arriving at a lesson to find that someone had looked at your exercise book and was trying – however clumsily and inadequately – to get you to produce something further was, I suppose, a signal to the Deptford adolescent mind that maybe, just maybe, this woman really did care a bit.

Pregnancy in the early 1970s was nothing like as well monitored as it is now. There were no pregnancy testing kits in chemists and supermarkets. I had to wait until I'd missed two periods and then present myself to my GP. He did an internal examination – long

144

since discredited as a sensible procedure in early pregnancy – and pronounced that I was 'about ten weeks'.

Thereafter I was assigned to a midwife and had to see her once a month until the sixth month of pregnancy. After that it would be fortnightly, and weekly in the final month.

Scans were in their infancy and used only in cases of extreme need. Few hospitals had them and fewer still had trained sonographers. The most sophisticated piece of equipment I saw throughout my first pregnancy was a traditional ear trumpet. The midwife or doctor would press the wide end on your distended abdomen and listen to the foetal heart by applying his or her ear to the other. Identical items of gynaecological practice have been found in Egyptian tombs.

At one point, Mrs Hedges, 'my' midwife, and the doctor suspected that my baby might be twins. They fumbled about, feeling and pressing my swollen belly and thought – or at least one of them did – that there might be two heads. So they sent me off to Lewisham Hospital for an X-ray to settle the argument.

There was just one baby.

X-raying a pregnant woman is now regarded as a very dangerous procedure because of the radiation risk to the baby. Today, if you're carrying a child, you'd be unlikely to get even your teeth X-rayed. Later in the pregnancy that same GP prescribed me barbiturates in the form of a drug called Soneril because I was having trouble sleeping. With hindsight it's a miracle that my child was, in due course, born as healthy as he was.

Ante-natal classes were patchy too and no one offered them to me. Of course I could have asked and attended some but chose not to. I was reasonably self-assured about the pregnancy and certainly didn't want clubby sessions with other pregnant women, so I made my own arrangements.

For example I got a couple of books out of the library which detailed the precise state of the baby's development as the months went by.

In school Geoff was about to show a film of childbirth to a class of fourth-year boys. 'Ooh, I've never seen that, can I come too?' I asked because he happened to have programmed it at a time when I wasn't teaching. So up I went and sat in the science lab with the boys. I knew many of them well from 1B days. They made me very welcome and were quite excited about my condition. And somehow I think my presence – a real pregnancy in the room – made their human biology lesson seem more real, relevant and important.

It was a black and white film without soundtrack – only voiceover explaining what was happening. So viewers were spared the worst of the blood and gore, not to mention the squelching and any loud expressions of discomfort which might have been emanating from the mother who, it has to be said, looked pretty uncomfortable.

But that didn't stop several boys from going green-faced and one, sensible Mark Shaw, fainting completely and falling off his lab stool with a loud bang. 'Can't stand the sight of blood, I expect,' said Geoff expertly scooping Mark off the floor into a sitting position. 'There's one in every class. This always happens when we show this film.'

Mark was a bit shamefaced about it afterwards. 'I thought it was an interesting film and it was silly of me to faint like that,' he told me later that day when I asked if he was feeling better. 'But I can't help it. I come over funny if I even think about blood.' Then he remembered his manners and, mature as ever, asked me politely, 'But did it help you, Mrs Elkin?'

Poor lad. If he ever married and fathered a family I doubted he would be much help to his wife in childbirth.

As for me, the time to start maternity leave was rapidly approaching and, just as it had when I married, that meant presents.

I know it was Geoff who organised the staff collection because he couldn't resist telling me that one colleague, whose wife also taught on the staff – and I hardly knew either of them – had given him a whole £5. My net salary at that time was still well under £100 a month. I could buy a week's food for Nick and me for about £4. We looked at, but didn't in the event buy, a new Renault 4 with room for carry cot and so on, which would have cost under £500. So that gift was astonishingly, touchingly generous. It was probably the equivalent of between £50 and £100 today.

I have no doubt Geoff himself chipped in freely too, as well as bullying his colleagues as only Geoff could and would. I ended up being presented with a cheque for £30 which was enough to buy two dozen top-quality terry towelling nappies – none of the modern, almost ubiquitous reliance on disposables in the early 1970s. I boiled them hundreds of times and they graced the bottoms of both my children.

With the other half of the staff cheque I bought a bright blue aquamarine ring set in 9-carat gold. It came from a shop (long since closed) in Canterbury where I had seen a good selection of semi-precious gemstones in interesting colours. Nick and I went down there especially that half term. I have it still and wear it a lot. I felt the staff cheque was partly a personal gift to me so I split it: half on the baby and half on something I could keep for myself.

Boys in many classes presented me with baby clothes, toys, cot bedding, infant toiletries and much more. A number of Deptford mums had clearly been consulted and taken their sons shopping.

The boy librarians must have decided that they wanted to give me a 'leaving' present rather than a baby gift. They bought me a compact – one of those delightful, old-fashioned, circular containers for face powder in your bag. The one they gave me has a pretty lid, enamelled with flowers. For a long time I used it – and thought of those boys every time I got it out – but few people use compacts anymore and modern face powder refills don't fit it. I have it safely though. It lives in a display cabinet in my sitting room.

CHAPTER THIRTEEN

Lucas Kenneth Elkin was born on 24 January 1972, at home in the front spare bedroom of our flat in Forest Hill.

Home delivery was almost unheard of in the 1970s but I had fond memories of my mother giving birth to my younger sister at home, over the shop, in 1953. That was my only real experience of a baby arriving in a family. Although, aged six, I was smoothly removed from the family home and taken to grandparents during the birth itself, I saw the new baby when she was half an hour old and my mother cheerfully sat up in bed and plaited my hair for school, so everything seemed very natural and normal – and, maybe, the way these things should be done.

I'd also heard many horror stories about depersonalising indignities heaped on women in hospital maternity wards. Complete shaving of all pubic hair, known in a different context as a 'full Brazilian', was routine and compulsory, for example. So was the enema at the onset of labour to clear the bowel for the convenience of medical staff.

There was also a tendency to treat women in labour as if they were dairy cows devoid of human thought processes. And it was normal to remove babies from mothers overnight and put them all in a night nursery together where they were bottle fed, regardless of the mother's wishes.

I discovered at first hand that all these things, and worse, were true when, four years later, I was obliged by a minor last-minute complication to go into a dreadful East Midlands hospital – it closed not long afterwards – for the birth of our second son, Felix. I was unnecessarily and painfully catheterised because, having not been allowed to drink anything for hours, I couldn't urinate to order during the birth. Then it was stitching without anaesthetic with my legs in stirrups.

They separated me from Felix for eighteen hours from within half an hour of the birth without ever giving me a proper reason. When two women washed me after the birth, they never spoke to me or stopped gossiping across me to each other. I might as well have been a dirty car or a bowl of washing up. And breastfeeding mothers were, frankly, just a nuisance.

So my decision to opt for a home birth in 1972 was retrospectively vindicated. It meant preparatory visits to the flat by Mrs Hodges who checked that we'd got everything suitably organised and issued me with a 'home birth pack' – including pads, bed protectors and so on.

And it all went remarkably smoothly and easily. I woke feeling odd in the early hours, got up and made tea, accidentally let the cats out of the kitchen and had to chase them round the flat – lumbering about like a porpoise which had swallowed a couple of footballs. We phoned Mrs Hodges at about 7am. She and her assistant were there before 9 and Lucas arrived at 11. The GP looked in afterwards, removing his cigarette from his mouth for long enough to do the single stitch I needed.

In those days, like almost everyone else in my family and Nick's, I used to smoke myself. So I wasn't fazed by the doctor smoking in my flat or near my baby. Only forty years later it is illegal in Britain to smoke in workplaces, restaurants and pubs. Very few smokers indulge even in their own homes. The people of Britain, and many other countries, have more or less accepted a completely new smoking etiquette. I think we sometimes forget just how quickly attitudes have changed. For the record, I finally gave up in 1977.

I had popped into school once or twice in late pregnancy just to say hello to people because it felt so unnatural not to be there every day. Geoff, determined to keep properly in touch with me, called at the flat for a cup of tea every Friday after school, which became the routine until we moved to the Midlands when Lucas was just two.

Once Lucas was born and I was up and about again I took him to Creekside Comp to introduce him to colleagues and boys. We'd worked through several different cars in the early years of our marriage, including a bright blue, ex-police Morris Minor. We now had a white Vauxhall Viva estate car with room for the pram which, rather cumbersomely, folded up but you had to take the wheels off – very different from the slick, lightweight, easily stowed baby transporters you see young parents with now.

So I packed the Viva with Lucas and the pram and set off for Deptford. Edith Bridges, usually so distant, cooed and wanted to hold him. So did Janet and Margaret and lovely Mrs Port. I've noticed many times since that when an employee takes a new baby to her place of work it's almost a ritual that he or she is passed, parcel-like, amongst nearly all female colleagues and, occasionally, a male one. It's a tribal thing. The new arrival has to be bonded with and welcomed.

The boys were fascinated too. 'You'll have to get telly now, Miss,' said one. 'You can't have a kid and not have telly for him to watch.' Another asked me whether I planned to let Lucas play football, which made me giggle as he was only about three weeks old and still wrapped in a shawl. 'I bet you'll teach him to read when he's about two and get him loads of books,' quipped one of the librarians with more foresight than he knew. Lucas was reading well at four and always had plenty of books. Today he works in a university library.

Cedric's comment was more serious. 'You know you can come back as soon as your six weeks are up, don't you, Susan,' he said. 'I can find you as much or as little part-time as you want and you could bring Lucas with you.'

The six weeks was a requirement, bound into those early maternity leave arrangements. In 1972, a woman who had had a baby was not permitted to work until six weeks had elapsed since the birth.

I had thought long and hard about the work question during the last months of my pregnancy. We had budgeted and planned to live on Nick's salary for a while. Although we would have to be very careful and there would be very little for extras, we could manage if I stayed at home to look after Lucas – a position very few young mothers, sadly, find themselves in today now that rents and property prices are so high.

But a few weeks at home taught me something about myself which I hadn't previously realised: I am a compulsive multi-tasker, hard-wired never to be satisfied with doing just one thing at a time.

Later I taught in schools all day and did hours of private coaching for extra money in my spare time. Then, in my thirties, I spent six years doing an Open University degree – to compensate for the lousy higher education I'd suffered at teacher training college – at the same time as teaching full-time and bringing up a family. When Nick gave up office work and, for several years, ran his own business, I worked hard within it to support him at the same time as teaching. Later still, I took up professional writing, which meant teaching all day and writing all evening – until I finally phased out the teaching after eleven years part-time.

The first sign of this split-focus tendency surfaced when Lucas was a few weeks old and Cedric was tempting me to do some part-time teaching. Wouldn't it be lovely to have just a few pounds a month of my own? Nick and I had never argued about money but I'd always loathed the idea of all money being completely communal. If I worked a bit, I wouldn't have to negotiate for the price of a lipstick or a pair of stockings.

How about something local rather than having to commute to Deptford? Maybe a couple of afternoons a week in a primary school? 'If that's what you want, I'll introduce you to a friend of mine, Mr Rowntree,' said the ever-helpful Cedric. 'He's Head of

Cranston Primary School, which isn't far from you, and I know he needs someone to help with a small group.'

If someone said that to me now, my first question would be, 'What sort of a small group? Why are they being withdrawn from class?' But, in 1972, I was still innocently impervious to the smell of rats and before Lucas was even six weeks old, I took myself off to visit Mr Rowntree, whose school was near the primary school I had attended myself and very much like it.

I suppose I had been warmly recommended by Cedric because Mr Rowntree fell upon me with great enthusiasm. The job, he told me, was to teach a group of about eight boys, aged between seven and eleven, withdrawn from several classes because their behaviour was making life very difficult for the rest of their respective classes.

These boys – it was a mixed school but the girls were better behaved, it seemed – were permanently withdrawn and taught by Mr Rowntree's deputy – in a ghastly, very small, former stone-floored cloakroom which still had hooks for coats along with sinks along one wall. The deputy needed some relief in order to carry out her other duties. Hence the decision to bring someone else in for just a few hours a week.

Fine, I thought. How difficult could 'little' boys this age be? I was used to hulking fourteen-year-olds, I reasoned naively. The answer was, very difficult indeed and this, my only ever foray into primary school teaching, turned out to be the worst teaching job I ever had.

Cedric had told Mr Rowntree that the promised deal was that I take Lucas with me. So, six weeks and one day after his birth, Lucas and I began taking ourselves to Cranston Primary on Tuesday and Thursday afternoons. My first worry was trying to keep the baby's fragile routines going – which meant feeding him as soon as I arrived at the school. The women on the staff coldly directed me to the only female lavatory to breastfeed. I also needed the pram for him to lie in and as the junior department was on the

152

second floor I had to ask for help in carrying it up. Such assistance was very reluctantly given.

I was loathed by the staff almost from my first appearance. I couldn't do the job. The boys ran rings round me. From troubled homes and treated like pariahs with status in school, they noisily refused to do anything I asked. And I simply hadn't a clue what to do with them.

My only supporter on the staff was Mr Rowntree. He tried to help me during my first two weeks before the Easter break. Then, during the Easter holidays, he had a heart attack and I never saw him again. The long-suffering deputy now had to run the school and to her, I was just an incompetent with a baby – just one more problem for her to deal with.

My mother-in-law overheard one of the Cranston Primary staff – a crabby, critical, set-in-her-ways older woman – complaining loudly in the hairdressers: 'And now we've got this useless young mother who brings a baby to school with her if you please! She can't do the job at all. I don't know what things are coming to.' Having this repeated to me wasn't exactly a confidence booster.

With hindsight, I can't see how it could possibly have worked. I had to keep an eye on a baby in a pram in the corner and I didn't trust 'my' little class of miscreants anywhere near him. So I couldn't really concentrate on either the teaching or the baby managing. I tried very hard and spent a lot of time at home between those sessions preparing individual work for the group because they were mixed in every sense. But nothing worked. If that had been my only experience of teaching I doubt that I would have remained in the profession for twelve months – instead of the three and half decades I eventually clocked up.

Before the summer half term I realised that I'd made a big mistake. For the moment I was only likely to be able to do anything useful as a teacher if I went back to where I was known and had some idea of how to do the job. So I rang the long-suffering Cedric.

To my relief he agreed that I could start back at Creekside Comp in September, taking Lucas – now six months old – with me.

Taking a baby to work with you was almost unheard of in the 1970s and seriously off-limits for a whole generation after that. Now, interestingly, at the time of writing, the government is trying to find ways of making it possible for more women to do just that. There are two reasons. First, the government wants to get as many people working as possible for economic reasons. Second, the cost of paid-for childcare is now so high that for many young or new mothers there is simply no financial incentive to work because everything they can earn goes straight to a childminder or nursery.

It will need a big change of mindset amongst employers. And any government which wants to pursue this policy will have an uphill struggle to persuade many bosses to think as laterally, and to be as accommodating, as Cedric.

Many changes had taken place in the eight months, most of a school year, that I hadn't been at Creekside Comp. Cedric's unification plans had continued to forge ahead.

All boys were now based in the Creek Road building. Only science was taught in the former Upper School building near New Cross station. That meant that Geoff was permanently based in the other building. He had also – his eye on retirement and a good final salary in a few years' time – at last agreed to become 'one of them'. He was now in charge of the Annexe which meant a place in the management team, a move he had resisted for so long. I didn't teach on Fridays, so he went on calling on Lucas and me for tea after school once a week so that he and I could catch up with each other, the gossip and do a bit of note-comparing.

Cedric had appointed a full-time librarian and converted the little-used top hall at Creekside Comp into a state-of-the-art, light, airy, spacious library with turnstiles and systems which would have put many a public library to shame. It must have cost many thousands.

Such major changes cost money. Obviously. But it wasn't a problem. ILEA seemed to be awash with cash, and schools could ask for extra finance. At the same time the school leaving age was about to rise from fifteen to sixteen, which meant hundreds more pupils in secondary schools for an extra year and there had to be facilities for them. Raising of the School Leaving Age (ROSLA) had been in preparation since 1964 and was finally implemented in 1972. A large pot of ROSLA money went to local education authorities from the Department of Education and Science, and Cedric got a quarter of a million pounds of it – probably the equivalent of say £2.5 million now.

My friendly little library room had now reverted to its original use as a classroom. So had the staffroom. There was now, courtesy of ROSLA, a smart new staffroom at the far end of the building – so far from the new library that anyone wanting to get from one to the other in a hurry would have needed roller skates. All mod cons too. Staff now had lockers for their possessions and tables where they could work in the staffroom. Creekside Comp was rapidly becoming unrecognisable.

Cedric directed that a timetable be put together especially for me, and it was, in comparison with what I'd struggled with the previous term in that bleak primary school, pretty easy stuff. Yes, it included some small group work. But this time they were backward readers. I simply heard them read, read aloud to them while they followed, talked to them about books and reading and generally gave them some attention. It was both straightforward and congenial.

For the first time I was also timetabled to teach some fourth-year examination classes – boys destined to take CSEs the following year. I used the *Art of English Book 4* – with a brief to get lots of written work from the boys because this newfangled 'coursework' was a key part of the exam.

Teaching is a bit like swimming or driving. You strive and struggle and exhaust yourself, in some cases for quite a long time.

Then one day you suddenly realise that you have lift off – you've swum a width or driven to the shops without having had to think about the mechanics. I clearly remember the moment with both swimming and driving.

I had a similar eureka moment with teaching. Working with one of those CSE classes, a boy – large and potentially threatening, had I encountered him three or four years earlier – asked me a perfectly sensible question about the work. I answered it. He thanked me and turned back to the task. Everyone else was purposefully getting on with the job in hand. Nobody was attention-seeking or even gazing out of the window. It was a calm and orderly working classroom. Suddenly I realised that I had a whole class of fifteen-year-olds entirely under my control. *Blimey*, I thought, *I've cracked it.*

While Lucas was still sleeping for longish periods during the day, I could more or less work his routines to fit into what I had to do in school. The afternoons were quite short at less than two hours after all. The classroom I taught in most, actually the former staffroom, had a large walk-in store room, with window, now used by the English department as stock-storing space. I would put Lucas – in the pram top – down for his rest in there and leave the door, a few feet from my desk, just slightly ajar so I could hear if he stirred or woke. It became a routine for boys to arrive at lessons and ask cheerfully, 'Is your baby in the cupboard, Miss?'

And then there was Sports Day. Just as Cedric had wanted a proper Speech Day in Goldsmiths' Hall, so he determined on an aspirational Sports Day – none of the old low-key stuff in Deptford Park. Instead he hired the Crystal Palace sports stadium, built to Olympics standards in the 1960s. Money no object, he chartered a train to transport the boys there. Geoff and I scoffed at Cedric's delusions of grandeur, partly because we shared a loathing of all sports but, with hindsight, perhaps it was a good experience for the boys.

The event fell on a Thursday in June. Since Thursday was one of my teaching days and I lived much closer to Crystal Palace than to Deptford, I simply walked there with Lucas, obligingly asleep, in his buggy. All staff were present so there was very little to do for those of us who didn't have tutor groups to supervise. Geoff and I spent most of the afternoon patrolling the stadium perimeter, with the buggy, pretending to police the exits – except for when we joined a handful of colleagues in the commentary box for a cup of tea.

Actually almost all the boys enjoyed the afternoon – it was gloriously sunny – and there were few, if any, attempts to escape. I think there was a general sense that there was a bit of status in being part of an event in the Crystal Palace stadium. They were too far from home to break out anyway. Most wouldn't have known where they were or how to get to anywhere else.

Instead we used that opportunity for Geoff to update me on the gossip. He was incandescent with rage.

Fred Tomlinson, the newish Head of English – actually my direct boss or 'line manager' as we would say now – had at last been rumbled. We'd known for months that the man was amiable but useless. Totally incompetent as an administrator, Fred had bungled every aspect of the Head of Department's job from the day he'd arrived two years earlier. Now he had lost – yes lost – all the CSE coursework for all the English groups. That was the last straw for Cedric who had relieved the man of his job and appointed a young woman to start in his place the following term.

Geoff's incredulous anger was that Cedric wasn't taking disciplinary action or attempting to get the offender off the payroll. Instead Cedric had 'found' the useless Fred a non-job, or sinecure, on the staff so that he could stay on indefinitely, just teaching a few lessons – on the same salary as before. An easy, face-saving solution, but hardly a fair or moral one. Geoff knew all of this, of course, because of his management role. It wasn't generally known to the staff. I think that was the most interesting Sports Day I ever attended in thirty-six years – but not for the right reasons.

Accommodating an infant in school became inevitably more difficult – although to my knowledge no Creekside Comp colleague ever complained or made me feel uncomfortable about it – as Lucas approached his first birthday. He was, inevitably, becoming more mobile and less in need of long naps. Perhaps the time had come to consider leaving him with somebody.

It wasn't an easy decision. Teachers in my generation were very thoroughly indoctrinated against leaving children with minders by a book called *Child Care and the Growth of Love* by John Bowlby (1953). It was strenuously enforced compulsory reading in teacher training colleges. Bowlby argued with passion that any child looked after by anyone other than his or her parents would be irreparably damaged.

But this was to be only for a few hours a week. And I eventually convinced myself that it couldn't really hurt. So I asked about for recommendations, bearing in mind that this was long before childminders had to be registered or inspected by Ofsted. It was a Creekside colleague who recommended Mrs McPherson who lived with her family in a flat at the top of a large old house in Blackheath. I liked her and her home was clean and businesslike. I started leaving Lucas there for the two afternoons I taught. He seemed quite happy about the arrangement, never crying when I dropped him off and relaxed when I collected him.

The problem was the journey. It could take me over an hour each way through slow-moving traffic to get Lucas to Blackheath and myself to Deptford, which seemed disproportionate for two hours' teaching.

So after a term of two afternoons a week at Creekside Comp, I asked Cedric if we could increase my hours to two full days. Ever prepared, it seemed, to do whatever I wanted in order to keep me on his staff, he agreed immediately.

For a year I worked two full days a week at Creekside, leaving Lucas with Mrs McPherson. It worked pretty well as an arrangement and I was really very sorry it came to an end.

And the end was unavoidable. Nick's employer, the Local Government Training Board, was based in Alembic House at Vauxhall when he'd started working for them back in 1969. It had since moved out – at a time when individuals and organisations were leaving London in huge numbers – to Luton. Nick had, for some time, been commuting daily to Bedfordshire, at his employer's expense, but was expected eventually to move to Luton or somewhere close to it – again with financial support.

We bought a house in Wellingborough in the autumn of 1973 and finally moved into it in December – which left me jobless. But only for three weeks. In mid-January I had a call from an independent school, run by a charity, for special needs children. It had been given my name by Northamptonshire County Council with which, without a lot of hope, I had registered as wanting some sort of part-time job. 'We know you've got a child of two and are new to the area, but we're desperate. We wouldn't mind if you brought him with you...' said the Head. By chance the pupils were all boys, partly because many of them had impairments such as Duchene muscular dystrophy which occurs much more often in males than in females. So there'd be plenty of the usual hormone-driven male angst and I could expect to feel at home... although that bit was implied rather than said.

Another desperate head. Another unlikely niche. And a sense of the cycle starting all over again.

EPILOGUE

In 1981, when Lucas was nine and our younger son five, I was teaching in a girls' secondary school in Kent. Nick had left the Local Government Training Board to start his own business and we had bought a house near my teaching job.

One evening in July, after school, I caught a train to Bromley South station where Geoff – still driving his trusty chestnut brown Morris 1000 estate – picked me up and drove me to Deptford for a party.

Creekside Comp, only eight years after I had left it, was to close. Numbers had dropped. Far fewer people with school-age children now lived in the area. Deptford was changing fast and the old community was vanishing. Demolition schemes meant that many families were being rehoused, usually further out of London, into Kent or Essex.

There was a disco in the hall, with a lot of boys from the past. I was able to grab a quick word with Mark Shaw, now twenty-three and a teacher himself. But the disco was far too noisy to talk much. A group of us ended up, as we always had after parents' evenings and other events, in The Duke over the road – still then an old Deptford boozer, trusty but unpretentious.

Jack Rowlands was there with Jess, to whom he was now married. He had just started in a headship in Surrey – a job he kept for only a year or two before retiring on full pension while still only around fifty. Geoff and I both knew that there must have been a very serious misdemeanour and another of those face-saving solutions so common in the 1970s and '80s. After his sudden 'retirement', Jack and Jess went to his home town, Southwold in Suffolk, to run a bed and breakfast establishment until he left Jess for someone he'd met at the golf club.

Cedric had retired in full glory three years earlier, handing over the Creekside Comp reins to another man who, as it turned out, did little more than preside over the school's demise. Cedric spent most of his retirement looking after his ailing wife who had developed motor neurone disease, which is why he wasn't at the farewell do in 1981. A few years later, a car lover to the end, he took her and a friend out to lunch. Uncharacteristically he lost control of the car and hit a wall. He turned to Mrs Flyte in the passenger seat and said, 'This will cost me my licence.' Then he died.

Geoff retired when the school closed and lived on until 2008. He and Coral sold their house in London and moved to a pretty town in Sussex. There they walked, took part in local history and music events and lived pretty sunny lives – until Coral succumbed to cancer while still in her sixties. Because he had something witty, forceful and apposite to say about almost everything I still think of him most days. His was a voice which takes more than death to silence.

The school building in Creek Road was taken over by Rose Bruford Drama School who ran it for several years as an annexe to its main premises in Sidcup. After that it stood sad and empty for some time. Then it was demolished.

If you walk or drive up Creek Road from Greenwich towards Bermondsey now there is no sign that the school ever existed. Instead the street is lined with glittering office blocks and flats for people who work across the river in Docklands. There's a row of shops at street level where the school railings once were, including a pharmacy named 'Rose' in recognition of Rose Bruford – pretty much on the site of those appalling lavatories. Small houses and maisonettes cover the space where Mike Churchill's plumbing shop stood and where the boys used to find feral kittens on the waste ground and bring them to me.

Only The Duke remains, dwarfed but defiant amongst the multi-storey edifices which surround it. More a gastropub than a beer and sawdust dive these days, but still hanging in there. Like the spirit of Deptford?